Handing Over

NLP-based activities for language learning

Neuro-Linguistic Programming

Jane Revell & Susan Norman

Saffire

PRESS

First published August 1999

Published by

Saffire Press
37 Park Hall Road
London N2 9PT
T +44 (0)20 8883 3445
F +44 (0)20 8444 0339
hugh@saffirepress.co.uk

Fax +44 (0)208 444 0339
email hugh@saffirepress.co.uk

Designed by Hugh L'Estrange
Printed in Great Britain by Ashford Colour Press, Gosport, Hants, England

ISBN 1 901564 02 9

Also by Jane Revell & Susan Norman *In Your Hands: NLP in ELT*

The authors and publisher welcome comments on this or their other publications.

Introduction

NLP is doing what we do better, and feeling better about what we do.

Many teachers who know about Neuro-Linguistic Programming and use it in their lives have said to us:

Yes, but ... *what do I actually* **do** *with NLP in the language classroom?*

We wrote *Handing Over* for them. It is the companion volume to *In Your Hands*, the introduction to NLP for teaching and learning. Both books are written for teachers (although we know of schools where *In Your Hands* is being used with advanced learners and companies where it is used on training courses). *Handing Over* is more specifically concerned with applying the concepts and teachings of NLP to the language classroom and contains practical lessons and ideas to use with language learners. It is written for the teaching of English as a foreign language, but most of the suggestions are relevant to the teaching of any language. Although many of the activities can be done without knowing about NLP, an understanding of the basic concepts will allow you to appreciate the reasons behind them and help students get more from them. We have not repeated the information from *In Your Hands*, although we have given a brief résumé of some of the key ideas where they provide a rationale for the activities.

The book is organised into sections corresponding to key concepts in NLP. All the activities have been used successfully by one or both of us (and others) in a variety of situations, with individuals and classes of between six and 60 teenagers, adults, trainers, teacher trainees, business people, and some of them with up to 700 teachers at a time. Although activities appear in one section, the holistic nature of NLP means that many of them could equally well come under a different heading. The contents list at the back of the book gives an overview, but the best approach is to read through and decide how you can best integrate activities into your teaching.

The language level? Well, it really depends on you, although we have suggested a possible level for most activities. Here is an example:

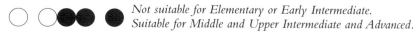
Not suitable for Elementary or Early Intermediate.
Suitable for Middle and Upper Intermediate and Advanced.

Our feeling about language teaching is that you grade the task not the language (or the students). Most of the activities can be used with students at middle intermediate level and above. Some are a bit more demanding, many are usable at lower language levels. Choose which you feel are most appropriate to your classes. The emphasis is on the meaning of the language. Vocabulary and structures are the vehicles needed to express ideas and we introduce them as students need them.

*Yes, but ... what do I actually **do** with NLP in the classroom?*

NLP is to do with method, not content. It is not a teaching method in the way that the 'direct method' or the 'Silent Way' are methods. NLP is an approach to life, learning and communication. Many aspects are directly or indirectly relevant to teaching. It's difficult to say which bits of the book are specifically NLP. Life levels, VAKOG and metaprograms, among others, are clearly NLP concepts, but at another level, anything that is good practice is NLP. Much of what is in this book is informed by years of good language teaching, and while the activities all exemplify our understanding of NLP, not all links have been made explicit. NLP validates what we are already doing well – albeit non-consciously. You are almost certainly practising NLP to some extent already. Greater knowledge of NLP will give you more options in your choice of approach.

There are five key ways in which NLP has helped us in our teaching.

- We have shared many aspects of NLP directly with students to make them better learners and better users of the target language.
- Tasks, strategies and exercises to enhance NLP skills can be used directly with language students or adapted for teaching the target language.
- Language is a key component of NLP and the NLP approach to language provides fascinating insights.
- Language teaching activities have been based on the various aspects of NLP.
- NLP has validated all the things we were already doing well and given us the confidence to continue. It has improved our relationship with students. It has improved our communication skills. It has stimulated our interest in how people learn, and helped us find some of the answers. Above all, it has reminded us of the differences between learners, and helped us view them as individuals with different needs – which is a lesson we cannot learn too often.

NLP has helped us to know and understand ourselves and other people better, and through this knowledge and understanding, in a wealth of different ways, to enhance the quality of our lives and the lives of others.

You'll find more answers to your questions in the 'yes, but ...' sections. Actually, we prefer to turn them into 'yes, ands ...'. There are several of them in the book, all responding to questions that practising teachers have raised.

For more information about what is in this book, we suggest you read it, in whatever order you find most appropriate. Certain activities and tasks build on what has gone before in the section, but they can be used independently, in any order, to supplement and enhance any teaching context.

When you have read through the book, we recommend that you continue to teach in your usual way. Start noticing the ways in which you are already incorporating ideas from NLP. Gradually introduce new ideas as appropriate. After about six months, review your own practice and the students' progress. Learn and gain confidence from your experience so far, and then be bolder!

If you could only take one message from this book, we would like it to be:

Teach the people – and the language will take care of itself.

Learning is finding out what
you already know.

Doing is demonstrating that
you know it.

Teaching is reminding others
that they know it
just as well as you.

You are all learners,
doers, teachers.

Richard Bach

What do you want from this book?

Why not make a note of your objectives here?
Write down precisely what you want.

Setting goals

'Knowing what you want helps you to achieve it' is a key NLP belief. The more clearly you know what you want, and the more clearly you express that goal to yourself and represent it in your mind, the more likely you are to be successful.

Writing it down, rather than just thinking about it, is important. In a thesis on goal-setting written at a university in the States in 1953, the author discovered that only 3% of the students had written lifetime goals. Those 3% were the ones who, 20 years later, were earning more than the rest of the class combined.

Earning lots of money may not be what you're after in life, but whatever your perceived goal, the principle is the same: be clear about what you really want, write it down very precisely, do whatever you need to do to move towards your goal ... and you stand a very good chance of success.

How can this apply in the language classroom?

As teachers, we can certainly use NLP strategies to clarify our own goals, and also to help students clarify theirs. The key to lesson planning is knowing exactly what you want to achieve – and marrying that with what students want to achieve. A good place for students to start is with the target language (which we assume is English).

- What do students want to achieve by the end of the course, the term or the year?
- Why are they learning English?
- What level do they want to achieve ultimately?
- How do they want to use their English?

If you are working in a secondary school, a possible response to the question *'Why are you learning English?'* is *'Because I have to!'* You can either introduce the concept of personal choice and responsibility, or you stand a better chance of enhancing students' motivation if you elicit and explore potential advantages with them ... but not like the teacher of French, who asked her 11-year-old pupils on their first day, *'Why are you learning French?'* Before they could answer, she put a transparency on the overhead projector and said: *'I'll tell you why. Here are the reasons! Copy them down in your notebooks.'* What a golden opportunity wasted!

The activities in this section are designed to get students thinking about their language-learning goals or career choice, or any other goals you might wish to explore with them.

The initial exercises help students identify what is important in their lives.

NOTE

We use the words 'goal' and 'objective' with students rather than the NLP word 'outcome', which has a slightly different connotation in everyday English.

PERSONAL PROFILE

Purpose

To help students decide on priorities and goals in their lives.

Language focus

Fluency; writing.

PROCEDURE

- Explain that the aim of the exercise is to produce a 'personal profile' of each student for a newspaper. Students answer the questions on the worksheet and then these are 'published'.

- Students work in pairs. One is the journalist who asks the questions. The other is the interviewee. The journalist writes down the answers. Then they swap roles. Responses can be jokey or honest – or a combination of the two. Students are allowed not to answer any two questions they choose.

- For homework everyone writes the profile of the person they interviewed. Profiles can be published in a class newspaper or displayed on the wall.

- When students see their own profiles, ask them to identify one thing they have learnt about themselves through doing this exercise. (They can decide whether or not they want to share this learning with others in the class.)

PERSONAL PROFILE QUESTIONNAIRE

What is your idea of perfect happiness?

What objects do you always carry with you?

Who or what is the greatest love of your life?

What is your greatest extravagance?

What is your greatest fear?

What personality trait do you most dislike in yourself?

What personality trait do you most dislike in other people?

What do you most dislike about your appearance?

What do you most like about yourself?

What is your favourite smell?

When and where were you happiest?

What is your motto?

What keeps you awake at night?

How would you like to be remembered?

What is the most important lesson life has taught you?

OBITUARY NOTICE

Purpose

To help students decide on priorities and goals in their lives.

Language focus

Past simple; writing.

PROCEDURE

- Explain to students that an obituary is a short newspaper article written about someone after they die and that they are going to write their own obituary. They write what they would like to see written about themselves.

  Since some students initially find this idea a bit shocking, it is worth spending time explaining more fully. Students can decide when and how they die – they can be 700 years old if they wish! The obituary can appear in the national news or in the local newspaper (or even a family circular letter). It can be as long or short as they like. They can write about their personal or professional life – whatever they want. The aim is to help them think about what they want to achieve in their lives.

- Students sit quietly and think about what they might write and make their first notes. They can then either write the obituary in class, or do it for homework.

- Students are given the opportunity to share their obituaries if they want to, either by putting them up on the wall or by moving round the class reading one another's. They are also explicitly given the option of keeping what they write private. This is one exercise that we don't correct unless students specifically ask us for help in phrasing, since the emotional investment can be quite high.

- Ask students individually to consider their obituaries in terms of their life objectives. What do they want to achieve in life?

- Then ask students to think about what they are doing now in terms of moving towards their life objectives. Ask them to write down three things they can do now to make their goals become realities. (Sharing these resolutions with a partner will help them commit even more to their chosen course of action.)

Comment

Although many people initially are unwilling to think about their own death, the exercise is very effective in helping them think positively about their life and most people come to realise this during the course of the writing. We never insist that people write an obituary, and if we meet with strong opposition, we offer the option of writing the speech someone makes about them on their retirement, or on their golden wedding anniversary, or their 100th birthday! (The basic tenses will then probably be a mixture of the past simple and the present perfect.)

Students write their obituary at a level they feel comfortable with. Some write a jokey obituary, while we have seen some extremely beautiful and moving pieces of writing resulting from this exercise.

If you know what you want,
you are more likely to get it.

NLP ADAGE

Purpose

To help students identify what they really want.

Language focus

Second conditional (or *will* future).

PROCEDURE

- Students work in pairs. They each write down a goal or something they want that they are happy to share with another person.

- Write on the board: *And if you got that, what would it do for you?*

- Explain that **A** will keep on asking **B** the question on the board, until **B** has been as precise as possible.

- At higher language levels, students can do the preparation exercise on the worksheet, to practise a question sequence which incorporates the previous answers. You can then ask for a volunteer to be questioned in front of the class, and elicit questions from the other students.

- Students then 'facilitate' each other in pairs (or in groups of three, with the third person being a helper to the other two). Give a time limit of five minutes each way, and extend it if necessary.

- At the end, students write a sentence linking their original goal with their final answer:

  If I got/get my goal, which is to _____ ,

  I would/will _____ .

- Afterwards, get class feedback of a very general nature on the process rather than the content of the activity. How do students feel after doing the activity? Did they discover anything interesting? Has their attitude towards their goal changed in any way? Do they feel more or less motivated now?

Variation

- The activity can be done using the certain future tense with 'when' instead of the tentative second conditional with 'if': *'And when you get that, what will that do for you?'* You might also ask students to use this future form immediately after doing the exercise in the second conditional. Ask them to notice whether the switch in tenses has the effect of making it more likely. Does that enhance their belief in it? Does it make it more scary? Do they have a better understanding of the difference between the future and the conditional in English?

- You could also do the exercise again, slightly altering the structure to: *'And what would speaking English fluently do for you?'*

ANSWERS TO WORKSHEET ON PAGE 11

2 And if you **spoke** English fluently ...; 3 And if you **felt** good about **yourself** ...; 4 And if you **had more confidence** ...; 5 And if you **were able to relax more with people** ...; 6 **And if you were able to take more risks**, what **would that do for you?** 7 **And if you learnt to do new things**, what **would that do for you?** 8 **And if you felt 'together' and in control of your life**, what **would that do for you?** 9 **And if you had a real sense of purpose**, what **would that do for you?**

WHAT WOULD THAT DO FOR YOU?

Fill in the gaps in this conversation between Amanda and Bernard.

1 **A** What do you want?
 B I want to speak English fluently.

2 **A** And if you _____ English fluently, what would that do for you?
 B I would feel good about myself.

3 **A** And if you _____ good about _____ , what would that do for you?
 B I would have more confidence.

4 **A** And if you _____ , what would that do for you?
 B I would be able to relax more with people.

5 **A** And if you were able to _____ , what would that do for you?
 B I would be able to take more risks.

6 **A** _____ , what _____ ?
 B I would learn to do new things.

7 **A** _____ , what _____ ?
 B I would feel 'together' and in control of my life.

8 **A** _____ , what _____ ?
 B I would have a real sense of purpose.

9 **A** _____ , what _____ ?
 B I would feel totally happy!

Yes, but ...

I really love all the ideas in your book and I really want to make them work, but I don't know how to begin. What can I do?

Yes, and ...

Start by writing down precisely what you want to achieve. Use positive language. Write what you *do* want, not what you don't want. Be very precise about the situations in which you want this, and the timescale (be realistic). Write down any of the smaller outcomes which might be steps on the way to your bigger outcome. You do not have to write how this outcome will be achieved, just be very precise and detailed about what you want.

When your outcome is exactly as you want it (it might take a few drafts), pin a neat copy somewhere where you can see it every day. Visualise yourself having achieved it. Make very clear pictures in your head. Then relax.

You can also ask your non-conscious mind for advice and then do one of the activities designed to harness its insights, or else just sleep on it. Whichever way you choose, once you have done it, open *Handing Over* at random, notice whatever idea jumps out at you and … plan it somehow into your teaching.

ACHIEVABLE GOALS

Purpose

To help students clarify an objective and therefore make it more achievable.

Language focus

Want, will.

PROCEDURE

- Ask students individually to write down a goal.
- They share their ideas with a partner.
- Explain to students that the way we express a goal to ourselves – the way we put it in words and think about it – makes it more or less achievable. The clearer and the more thought-out the goal, the better. They work with a partner through the worksheet checklist of questions on the next page.
- Students write the final version of their goal on a sheet of paper, put their name on it and hand it in to you. You could then:
  - look at what they have written, keep a record and hand them back – giving individual advice on improvements and follow-up where necessary.
  - put the papers up on the noticeboard or wall (with agreement) so everyone can read each other's and offer support and advice.
  - read them out anonymously, pausing to allow people to offer support and advice.
  - suggest they pin up their goal somewhere prominent where they will see it every day.
  - do a combination of the above.

Comment

This activity can be done in English with an advanced or intermediate group. Lower level monolingual classes can initially write their goals in their mother-tongue. Then they ask each other and the teacher to help them express what they want to say in English.

> 'Would you tell me please, which way I ought to go from here?'
>
> 'That depends a good deal on where you want to get to,' said the Cheshire Cat.
>
> 'I don't much care where …' said Alice.
>
> 'Then it doesn't matter which way you go,' said the Cat.
>
> Lewis Carroll, *Alice's Adventures in Wonderland*

ACHIEVABLE GOALS

What is it that you want? Write one of your goals (large or small) here:

As you work through the questions, refine and rewrite your goal as necessary. At some point, you may decide that you don't really want this goal after all. That's a useful thing to find out! You can start the exercise again with a different goal.

Make sure that your goal is written in a positive way, that it is what you *do* want, not what you *don't* want!

> *I don't want to mispronounce words. (✗)*   *I want to pronounce words intelligibly. (✓)*
> *I want to avoid making mistakes. (✗)*   *I want to speak correctly. (✓)*

How will you know when you've achieved your goal? What exactly will happen? Be precise, eg *I will pass my X exam. At the end of this term, I will get a grade X or above. When I speak to my English friend, she will understand me easily. I will understand the story and about a third of the words when I watch an American movie.*

Precisely when, where and with whom do you want this goal to be effective? You might want to 'be more assertive' with sales people, for example, but not with your friends.

Is there anything you will lose if you achieve this goal? Write here what you might lose and then decide whether the advantages still outweigh the disadvantages.

Is achieving this goal within your control? If it depends on other people, you might have to work much harder to achieve it. If it depends on changing other people, you might never succeed!

I want other people to pay attention to me. (✗)   *I want to have more impact. I want to make myself more noticeable. (✓)*

What are you already good at that can help you? What resources and skills do you have that make you more likely to succeed in achieving your goal?

What do you need that you don't yet have?

How can you get anything else you need?

Can you experience your goal clearly in your mind? Can you see, hear and feel what it will be like in the future when you have your goal? If not, make sure you really want this goal, look back over the previous steps and rewrite your goal.

Purpose
To give students practice in challenging goals.

Language focus
Question forms.

PROCEDURE

- Give students the worksheet to work through in small groups. You might give different goals to different groups, or start different groups in different places on the worksheet.

- Two students state each goal and try to improve it in response to challenges from the others. All challenges must be in the form of questions. The only ban is on questions beginning with 'Why'. (Why-questions encourage students to defend and hold onto a goal rather than to challenge it.)

- To check that the goal is well formed, everyone tries to imagine themselves in the position of the person whose goal it is.

- When the group is confident that the goal is well formed, they write down the final version and move onto the next.

CLARIFY YOUR GOALS

Look at these goals. Which ones are well formed (ie expressed in such a way as to help the person achieve that goal)? Restate the goals which are not well formed.

1   I want to leave home. _____

2   I don't want to leave home. _____

3   I want a lot of money. _____

4   I want to live near my parents. _____

5   I like singing. _____

6   I want my parents to stop hassling me. _____

7   I want to be earning £250,000 per year
   by the time I am 30. _____

8   I want to get a job. _____

9   I want people to like me. _____

10   I want to understand English. _____

11   I want my pronunciation to be easily
   understood by native speakers. _____

Purpose

To help students overcome their negative perceptions.

Language focus

Could; future perfect (or *will* future); writing.

PROCEDURE

● Students take a new, clean piece of paper and write down a well-formed goal.

● Below the goal, they write the word 'OBSTACLES' and then list as many things as possible which make the goal difficult (or impossible) to achieve. They should write all sorts of objections to do with material and physical problems (eg no money) as well as personal qualities which they feel are lacking (eg self confidence). They write clearly on one side of the paper only and number each objection. (If they come to the end of the paper, they start a new clean sheet for further obstacles.)

● When students run out of ideas, they work in groups of three or four and try to think of more obstacles for everyone's goals.

● Working alone again, students look at the obstacles and think of ways to overcome them. On the other side of the paper, they write two or three possible ways of overcoming each obstacle, beginning, *I could …*

● When students run out of ideas, they work in their groups again until they have at least one suggestion for overcoming each obstacle. If anything is really difficult to overcome, ask everyone in the class to offer suggestions (beginning, *You could …*, or *Maybe you could …*).

● When students have their completed lists, they read through the positive suggestions and identify priorities and things they can and will do now or in the near future. On a new sheet of paper, they write their goal again and write an action plan. They list the things they will do, with a timescale, using the future perfect, eg *By 30 July, I will have saved £1,000*.

At lower language levels, students can express their determination using *will*, eg *In the holidays I will get a job to earn some money*. The final line reads, *By (date), I will have achieved my goal*.

SUGGESTED ANSWERS TO WORKSHEET ON PAGE 14

1 (Say what you're going towards, not what you're moving away from.) 2 I want to live at home with my parents for at least another year until I've finished my exams. 3 (Say what you want the money for.) 4 I want to live within a five-minute walk of my parents' home while they are able to look after themselves. 5 I would like to sing regularly with other people in a choir which performs to the public. 6 (Say how you will need to behave in order to affect your parents' behaviour. Say what you want your parents to do, not what they shouldn't do.) 7 Fine. (Is the precise amount of money important? Could it be more? What sort of job would you like to do to earn this money? Are you prepared to do anything?) 8 (What sort of job? Be as precise as possible.) 9 (Which people? How will you know they like you? How will they behave?) 10 (What precisely do you want to understand? Books? Films? Teachers? The whole grammatical system?) 11 Fine (Now what do you need to do to improve your pronunciation?)

DOODLE A DREAM

Purpose

To help students think about their long-term goals.

Language focus

Adjectives.

PROCEDURE

- Students have a clean piece of paper and a pen or pencil ready. Pre-teach the word 'doodle'.
- Ask students to sit quietly and comfortably, close their eyes and go inside.

Just let your mind relax, and think forward ten or twenty years to imagine yourself in the future. What do you want your life to be like? How do you want to feel? What sort of things do you want to be doing? What sort of things will you see around you? What sounds will you be hearing? Just let your mind roam over your professional life, your job, your career, your work. And your personal life, your relationships, your parents, maybe children, grandchildren. Your home. Travel. Holidays. Your leisure activities. Anything you would like to have in your future. And then keeping those thoughts, pictures, sounds and feelings in your mind, come back to the classroom, pick up your pen and doodle. Just draw any shapes that seem to represent your future.

- Students quietly draw their doodles.
- After a few minutes, students get together in small groups to look at their doodles and think about what they mean (groups of four and five can be formed as students finish). Ask students to say what they see in other people's doodles, rather than explaining their own (although that is likely to happen too).
- When everyone is in groups and has started looking at the doodles, ask them to stop for a moment and concentrate on you. Ask them to think about what sort of things to look for in the doodle and what it might mean. Are the lines hard or soft? Thick or thin? Dark or faint? What does that indicate? Are the shapes curved or straight? Closed or open? Rounded or sharp? Big or small? Is the picture unified or made up of lots of different things? Clean or messy? Elicit what people think these might indicate? (Remind them that this is not to be taken too seriously, but just to respond to what they see.)
- Continue with the group discussions about the doodles.
- Ask students whether anyone has learnt anything new about what they want in life. (They don't necessarily have to say what they have learnt.) Ask them to think of one thing they could do now to make sure this future will happen.

Purpose

To help students think about their skills and behaviour in different contexts.

Language focus

Qualities; present simple.

PROCEDURE

- Students work in groups to brainstorm ideas onto a large sheet of paper in relation to their own lives under the main 'life levels' categories:
  - Think of all the **environments** you operate in, all the places you habitually frequent, eg kitchen, lounge, bedroom, classroom, sports club, office, client's offices, friends' houses (different situations with different friends), dentist, car, etc.
  - Think of your **behaviour** in all these different places, all your different roles, eg cook, patient, tennis player, secretary, publicity officer, musician, audience member, mathematician, etc.
  - Think of all your different **abilities** (both practical skills and personal qualities), the things you are able to do which allow you to behave in particular ways in one or more of the environments, eg efficiency, sense of humour, computer skills, kindness, ability to ride a bike, cooking skills, good spelling, etc.

- When everyone has brainstormed a lot of ideas, they move around the room to look at the ideas other groups have come up with.

- Hand out to each group about fifteen cards in each of three colours (45 cards in all per group). These need only be big enough to write individual words on and can be made by cutting up sheets of paper (or card).

- Each group creates their own life levels cards: writing ten key environments on one colour, ten behaviours on another colour, and ten abilities on the third.

- Students take turns in taking three cards, one of each colour. They justify to the others why they are behaving in that way in that place and how that ability enables them to do it. This may call for a little ingenuity. If the others accept the explanation, they award one, two or three points. The person with the most points is the winner after a set number of rounds or at the end of a time limit.

Follow up

- Suggest to students that they write similar cards for their own lives and play the game, thinking about their own behaviour and skills in the different roles they play in their lives. They might enjoy a private discussion about themselves with a partner in English, but we would never pressurise anyone to reveal personal information in a language classroom. You might also point out to them the other three 'life levels':

Belief What are all the things that I believe about myself, about the way the world is, the way society operates, the way people do or should behave?

Identity Taking into account everything I know about myself, what is it that makes me 'me'? Who am I? Which things stay the same and which things change in different circumstances or might change over a period time?

Spirit What is there beyond myself that I believe in? It may be a spiritual belief, or a cause that I would work for or which is in the interests of humanity, or it may be a driving force beyond myself.

Purpose

To review one's goals and outcomes in a different way to make sure they are congruent with all aspects of one's life.

Language focus

Any.

PROCEDURE

♦ Students work in pairs to review goals they have written (see pages 13-15). One person clearly states (or writes down) their goal. Their partner guides their thinking and the discussion by working through a list of questions on a worksheet. Not all the questions will be relevant to all goals.

Environment What kind of places do you imagine yourself in, when you've got this goal? Where will you be able to put this goal into practice? Where will it be useful? Are there any places where it would not be useful?

Behaviour What sorts of things will you be doing when you've achieved your goal? How will this goal help your behaviour? Which things do you do now that you will do better when you have achieved your goal? Is there anything you do now that will be worse if you achieve this goal? Is there any negative behaviour which will result from this goal?

Capabilities What qualities, skills, experience and knowledge do you already have that will help you move towards your goal? Do you need anything in addition to all of these? If so, how will you go about getting what you need? What qualities, skills, experience and knowledge are likely to be enhanced by achieving your goal? Are there any qualities or skills which will be lost or under-used once you have achieved the goal? Are there any new skills or qualities you are likely to acquire along with this goal?

Beliefs What positive beliefs do you have about yourself and other people that support you in this goal? Do you have any beliefs which might stop you achieving this goal? Do you have any beliefs which might be compromised if you achieve this goal? Which beliefs do you have which might be enhanced by achieving this goal? Do you think you might gain new beliefs as a result of achieving this goal?

Identity How does this goal fit in with your identity, your sense of who you are? How does it fit in with the many different roles or identities you have in your life? Do you see any threat to your sense of identity if you achieve this goal?

Spirit How does this goal fit in with the overall purpose of your life, your sense of what your life is all about? Does your goal enhance your sense of purpose, mission and spirit? Does your goal in any sense detract from it? Will your sense of spirit or purpose help you achieve your goal?

Comment

These questions help students clarify important issues and think through the implications of achieving goals. They may also throw up potential problems and objections. Anything 'negative' is to be welcomed, not feared: it provides useful information which will enhance the likelihood of success.

Class feedback can centre on the activity rather than the content, eg by asking students which questions were most interesting, most worrying, most enlightening, etc.

Guided Fantasy: Climbing a mountain

And as you set off up the mountain, full of energy, full of hope, full of expectations, remember that the longest journey begins with a single step. Have in your mind an image of what it will be like when you get to the top, what you will see, what you will hear, what you will feel ... and allow that image to sustain you along the way.

And as you walk, look around you and enjoy what you can see: the colours, the shapes, the textures, listen to the sounds you can hear, feel a sense of purpose and expectation. You know it's a long way up, and you trust that you're going to make it. Trust yourself.

And as you walk up, you may like to think about an important goal in your life right now. Think about the places where you'll be when you've got what you want. See, hear and feel what that will be like.

And as you continue walking up, imagine yourself doing the things you'll be doing in those places and how you will be enjoying it. What do you see, hear and feel that's different?

You're aware that the walk is becoming a bit steeper now, but you're doing fine, as you think about all the skills and knowledge and resources and experience that you have that will help you reach the top, and all the skills and knowledge and resources and experience that you have that will help you reach your goal.

And as you walk it's getting a bit steeper and a bit harder, but remember that it's also getting a bit easier because you know that with every step, you're moving nearer your destination.

And you realise you're about half-way up now, and you may like just to stop for a moment and turn around and look back and see how far you've come already. Be glad about that, and let that sense of achievement strengthen you in your resolve to go on.

And now when you're ready, go on walking up and up, and as you do so, have a sense of all your positive beliefs that support you in what you want.

And just for a moment, experience who you are. Who you are right now, how you are changing, how you will be different as you achieve what you want to achieve.

It's getting very, very steep now and you may be feeling tired. Remember that we often feel most exhausted when we are close to success. Experienced mountain climbers know this. Know that this is the moment to make a final effort, because you are very close to the top. Close to success. To help you at this moment, recapture once more the image of what it will be like when you get to the top. What it will be like when you succeed.

▶▶▶

When you are ready, take a deep breath and walk on, allowing a sense of the spirit of your life to flow through you as you do so, merging with the important goal that you have in your mind.

And walk up and up and up until, finally, you take the last two or three steps as you reach the top of the mountain.

Look around you, far and wide, and delight in everything you see. Listen to the sounds … or the silence … and delight in everything you hear. Feel a sense of exhilaration and achievement and delight in that too. Allow the achievement of your important goal to be in your mind at the same time. And enjoy it all. And feel glad.

And you might like to allow a word or a picture to come into your mind that somehow symbolises this sense of success. And know that whenever you recall your word or picture, the sense of success will come back to you and strengthen and support you in your endeavours.

So slowly, in your own time, and whenever you're ready, take a few deeper breaths and gently stretch and open your eyes and come back, softly and gently, into this room, into the here and now.

I know that look, Malcolm ~ you're up that mountain again, aren't you?

Come to your senses!

The representational system in NLP says that we experience the world through our five senses: Visual, Auditory, Kinaesthetic, Olfactory and Gustatory (known as VAKOG). Most people tend to have a preferred sense (or two) for taking in information, ie they tend to *see* it (V), *hear* it (A), or *do something* with it (K). (We haven't yet come across anyone over the age of five who prefers their main experience of something to be through the sense of taste or smell!) This does not mean, however, that we should label students or ourselves as *being* their preferred sense. Statements such as 'I am a visual', 'He is auditory', can be very limiting. NLP seeks to give people more options, not fewer.

Most students can take in information through any sense, but in any class, about a third of our students are likely to have a preference for one of the three principal senses. For a few, it makes a significant difference to their progress. The important thing is to present new language in a variety of ways to cater for all learning styles.

It is useful to know your own preferred style, since that is how you are likely to present material 'automatically' – when you're busy or don't have much preparation time. This tends to favour only some of your students. It is useful for students to know their own preferred style, so that they can make the most of their strengths. The easiest way to find out each student's preferred learning style is to tell them what the options are and then ask them. Most people know.

We make VAKOG explicit to all students. When teachers and students know their strengths, they can then work on and develop the senses they use less readily, in order to maximise learning potential. Teaching and learning will improve from the greater diversity, and people often notice an added richness in their everyday lives.

Most English language teachers are already taking account of the three main systems (V, A and K) when they present information. NLP is simply validating good practice. However, knowing about VAK may help us remember consciously to vary our classroom activities a little more. As with so many things in NLP, being more flexible leads to more choices and greater effectiveness.

Processing information

There is a second and different aspect to VAKOG, however. So far we have been considering how people *take in* information through their senses. One of the ways we *process* information also uses our senses. Other ways depend on our metaprograms (see page 64). We see internal pictures when we visualise or imagine (image-ine), and we hear sounds inside our heads. (Most of us are aware of our 'inner voice' when we talk to ourselves, and have had the experience of a song or tune which we get 'on the brain'.) We also feel things internally, both as emotions and as physical sensations, eg butterflies in the stomach, or a tightening of the chest. Internal smells and tastes are also possible, although these systems operate in a different way within the brain.

Most people use all three main senses when they process information, but individuals do so in different ways and in different sequences. People are generally much less likely to know 'automatically' what their *sequences* and *strategies* are. (See modelling, page 107 onwards.)

One interesting point to note is that most people cannot easily use a sense externally and internally at the same time. You can only visualise or see internal pictures if you close or defocus your eyes. It's almost impossible to remember the tune of one song while actively listening to another. Similarly, it's very difficult to imagine a smell or a taste while actually sniffing or tasting something else. The kinaesthetic situation is a bit different, because an external touch can certainly be experienced at the same time as an internal emotion and we personally think we can imagine touching one thing (eg cold water) with one hand while actually touching something else (say, hot water) with the other. Try it!

From a teaching point of view, the important thing is sometimes to give students a lot of sensory input, particularly when presenting new information, and sometimes to give none: let them use their imaginations.

Because we use all our representational systems simultaneously, it is practically impossible to suggest exercises which focus exclusively on one particular sense. So we have given some suggestions for activities which relate principally to V or A or K, and others which enhance awareness of all three.

SENSORY LANGUAGE

Purpose

To raise awareness of the language related to the senses, and the way it is used.

Language focus

Different parts of speech connected to the senses.

PROCEDURE

◆ Ask students to sort the words and sentences on the following page into a table connected to the senses. They can work individually or in pairs or groups, or the task can be set for homework.

◆ Students compare their tables, discuss how the words are used and create new example sentences.

Comment

The trick with example sentences is to think of a specific situation in which you might want to say something connected with the senses, rather than thinking simply of the grammatical form. Remember that the senses are connected with both our external awareness and our internal processing, and example sentences might reflect this. Also note that many examples of 'sensory' language might be metaphorical, rather than specifically descriptive, eg That smells fishy! It sounds a bit iffy to me!

I heard that!   tongue   What can that dog smell?

They looked at the pictures.   How do you feel about that?   smell

see   listen to   taste   Taste this!

They looked at the pictures.   She's watching TV.

                        He saw her.

feel   Your story really touched me.

It feels right to me.   It touched the ground.   taste   touch

It touched the ground.   nose   Listen to me!

It sounds awful.   hearing

                    It looks as if we're leaving now.

What's that smell?   It tastes delicious.

It sounds as if you need to stop.   Feel how silky this is.

He looks like his father.   ear

vision   It feels as if my life is just beginning.   She looks happy.

What a beautiful sight.

sight   I've got a very strong feeling about this.   hear   This rose smells lovely.

You have such a gentle touch.   eye   Did you hear that sound?

                        watch

It didn't sound like her.   It tastes a bit like chocolate.

                look at

His handshake feels like a dead fish.   It smells like new-mown hay.

                        The taste is hard to describe.

skin   It tastes as if it needs more salt.

It smells as if something's going bad.

FROM SENSE TO SENSE

Purpose
Enhancing sensory awareness.

Language focus
Descriptions: *look/smell/sound/feel/taste like.*

PROCEDURE

● Ask students to work in groups and describe their experience of colours in different senses. They ask and answer questions such as:

A *What does 'green' smell like?*

B *It smells like wet grass. It smells minty.*

B *What colour is the ringing of a church bell?*

A *I think it's deep, rich brown.*

SENSIBLE SAM

Purpose
To highlight sensory language.

Language focus
Reading comprehension.

PROCEDURE

● Give students a copy of Sensible Sam's Problem Page (next page). Individually or in pairs or groups, they identify which person is experiencing the problem in a visual, auditory or kinaesthetic way.

● Once they have agreed which is which, students identify the specific words and expression relating to the sensory experience.

● More advanced students could then write letters from Sam in answer to each of the letters, trying to match the sensory language.

Suggestions for replies from Sensible Sam

Dear Pat I do understand how you feel. It must be very uncomfortable to be under so much pressure. You're obviously very in touch with your feelings. Why don't you grasp the nettle with both hands? Lay your cards on the table. Be honest about how you feel. Your friends would be very inflexible and insensitive not to respect your feelings. (K)

Dear Sean Your situation does not sound very harmonious. Perhaps you need to listen to your dad and give him a fair hearing too. In order to have more harmony at home, maybe you need to talk about some kind of compromise. For example, working part-time would give you time to play your music. Listen to your feelings. Something will ring true! I look forward to hearing from you. (A)

Dear Wendy I get the picture. You paint a very clear picture of the situation. Even though it's staring Lucy in the face, I can see how difficult it must be to get her to see the light without destroying her illusions. Perhaps you could look at it in another way. Rather than focus on Harry not liking Lucy, focus on him liking someone else. Could you take another point of view? I hope to see you sometime. (V)

SENSIBLE SAM'S PROBLEM PAGE

Dear Sensible Sam

Recently all my friends have had their noses pierced. Now they're talking about having their belly buttons done. They're putting a lot of pressure on me to have mine done too, but the idea leaves me completely cold. I'm afraid of the pain – even having an injection makes me go weak – and I don't think I could stand the feeling of having something up my nose all the time, especially when I've got a cold. Just the thought of it turns me right off!

How can I get through to my friends to make them leave me alone and stop pushing me?

Pressurised Pat from Peterborough

Dear Sensible Sam

I am nineteen years old and left school two years ago. Since then I've been practising my singing and my music so I can play in a band one day. My dad keeps yelling at me and telling me to get a job. I hear what he's saying but I really need time – and some peace and quiet – to think through what I want to do with my life. When I try to discuss it with him he seems to go deaf and just refuses to listen to me. Does his attitude sound reasonable to you? Please tell me what to say to him to convince him.

Shouted-at Sean from Sheffield

Dear Sensible Sam

My best friend, Lucy, is mad about my friend, Harry, and has this vision of their brilliant, sparkling future together. The trouble is though, that Harry finds Lucy really unattractive, in fact he can't stand the sight of her. Even though this is crystal clear to everyone else, Lucy refuses to see it. If she goes on imagining a relationship with Harry in this way, she's going to be very disillusioned.

How can I help open Lucy's eyes so she gets a clearer perspective on things?

Can you shed some light on this problem?

Watchful Wendy from Weymouth

Taking account of students' need for ...
VISUAL input

Diagrams   Real objects   Comics   Write words up HIGH

Posters   Acting out   Shape   Colour

Pictures   Mime   Wall displays

Mind Maps   Video   Photographs

White space   Page layout   Picture books   Tidy room

Visualisation   Inner pictures   Drawing

Charts   Clear, uncluttered work

Writing   Facial expressions

Overheads   Slides   Flip charts   Beauty   Films

Tracing in the air   Visual jokes

Gestures

Write words in groups   Writing in different sizes and colours for IMPACT   Write words on board/on walls

Add your own ideas to this page.

Yes, but ...

I like these activities, but I have to use a coursebook.

Yes, and ...

- Use the coursebook as the source of the content of what you teach and for homework activities. Use *Handing Over* as the source of ideas for how you teach that content.
- Open your coursebook at random and choose an exercise. Open *Handing Over* at random and find something on the page which you could incorporate into the coursebook exercise.
- Look through the coursebook and make notes as to how and where you could incorporate ideas and specific activities from *Handing Over*.
- Take five ideas that you really like from *Handing Over* and adapt them for the language you intend to teach in the next two weeks.

Visual discrimination

The following exercises rely on and practise visual discrimination. They can all be adapted for any level.

How many letters?   Take any paragraph from a part of a textbook students will not actually be studying for a week or two. Ask them to find as many examples as possible of a particular letter or word, eg *How many letter 'a's can you see in this paragraph? How many capital letters are there? How many vowels are there? What is the first example of the letter 'I'? How many times does the author use the word 'but'?* (Students will pick up some awareness of the text peripherally which will make it seem more familiar when they come to study it later.)

How quickly can you find …?   Help students find their way round a new textbook, reader or dictionary, by calling out things for them to find, eg

What's the first word on page 32?

On which page is the picture of the mountain?

How many times does the word 'the' appear on page 17?

What is the title of the story on page 57?

On which page is the story of Asclepius?

How many paragraphs are there on page 29?

When students find the answer they stand up, and you give them a number (ten to the first, nine to the second, etc), which becomes a countdown. When you reach zero, ask students to call out the answer all together on the count of three.

Internal pictures   Students' imaginations provide an endless and fasacinating supply of experiences which can form the content of language activities which will have an in-built motivation factor. Check or input core vocabulary using any picture from the textbook. Ask students to relax and go inside and imagine a similar sort of picture as they would like it to be, eg my ideal seaside, my ideal garden, my ideal house. Students then work in groups or pairs to describe their own pictures to one another.

Walk like a blind person   Students work in pairs. **A**s are blindfolded (or simply shut their eyes), **B**s are the guides. It is helpful for the 'blind' person to have a stick or ruler, though this is not essential. For five minutes, using only verbal advice, **B**s guide their partners around the building (if possible) or just around the classroom (if not). The guide's role is to protect their partner from danger or mishap, and as far as possible they should not interfere with **A**'s exploration. In order for **A**s to do this successfully, they have to rely heavily on their internal pictures and memories, together with their external auditory and kinaesthetic systems (including the voice and touch of their partner).

After a few minutes, **A**s remove their blindfolds and recreate their walk, explaining what they experienced. **B**s can also add anything they noticed.

As and **B**s then change roles.

Students meet back and discuss the experience.

Mental photos   Students work in pairs. **A**s are blindfolded (or simply shut their eyes), **B**s are the guides. The **B**s guide the **A**s around the classroom, or (if possible) round the building or grounds. As they walk, **A**s use internal pictures, external sounds and sense of touch to imagine where they are. Every so often they stop, and **B** places **A**'s head in such a position that they will have a particular view when they open their eyes. **B**s then tell **A**s to open their eyes, look for a moment and then blink, mentally photographing whatever they see. The activity continues until **A** has taken four or five such 'photographs'. **A**s and **B**s swap roles.

The class meet back together and discuss the experience and the 'photographs' they took. Which was their most interesting photograph? Which one did they like least? Did what they saw match what they expected to see each time?

Spot the difference   Use spot-the-difference pictures from a children's comic book (or the examples on the next page). Students describe their pictures to one another to identify differences. Remember to identify similarities too.

Complete the picture   Photocopy a simple picture. White out different lines from the resulting pair of pictures (or use the ones on the next page). Give them out to pairs of students. Without looking at each other's picture, the students describe and draw to create identical pictures.

Optical illusions   Use any optical illusions or odd pictures (like these ones). Give different examples to students. Without showing their partner, they describe the picture without identifying what the visual oddity or illusion is. Their partner has to visualise the picture that is being described and guess what the illusion is.

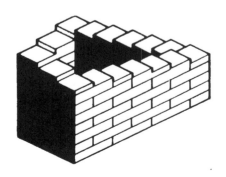
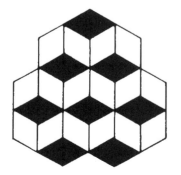

Spot the difference

Complete the picture

Pandora's box

Like most teachers, we both have a box in which we collect pictures, quotations, proverbs, jokes, sayings, advertisements, stories, old calendars, brochures, postcards, photographs, 3D pictures, puzzles, cartoons, 'spot the difference' pictures from comics, visual oddities, etc. Anything that appeals to us. Some of it relates directly to language learning, some of it doesn't. Some of it is double sided, some single sided. Some of it is mounted beautifully on card and laminated, some of it is scrappy and torn. Where there are words, most of them are in English, but some are in other languages.

If we need a larger number of pictures, we bring in a big pile of magazines, catalogues and brochures for students to search through to find their own. We don't have class sets, just one or two examples of each item. If something is particularly relevant to the whole class, one student can present it to the others. We use the box for a wide range of activities. Our overall aim is to practise language which is relevant and motivating to different individuals. The focus is obviously visual, and many of the activities also involve moving around, which helps kinaesthetic learners. We can bring in other senses by asking students to choose pictures and say what sounds, smells, feelings and tastes they are reminded of.

Visual display

- We put a variety of items on the wall for a changing display to create visual interest in the classroom. We often find students talking together about different items, copying down things which interest them, and initiating conversations with us about things on the wall. Whether or not students take an active interest in items, they will take in information peripherally.

- You can also display pictures relating to a forthcoming topic or language item.

Introducing a topic

- As a way of introducing a topic, put out a lot of different items from the box. Give everyone two minutes to find an item which relates to the given topic. If they can't find anything directly related to the topic, encourage them to be inventive in their explanation of why something is related.

- Alternatively, or subsequently, divide the class into teams and give everyone two minutes to find an item which is *not* related to the topic in any way. Other teams can challenge if they can give a satisfactory explanation as to why an item *is* in fact related to the topic.

Alphabet vocabulary

- Teams are given a letter of the alphabet each (good letters are P, C, S, T, M, B and D). They collect as many pictures as possible containing vocabulary beginning with that letter and arrange them on a large sheet of paper, while keeping a separate (secret) list of the words.

    Groups go round, making lists of all the items they can see on each sheet. Then different groups score one another, checking against the original lists.

I like it

♦ Put out a lot of items from the box. Give everyone two minutes to choose one item they really like. They then get into groups of four and each person says why they really like their item At lower language levels, write the basic sentence pattern on the board: *I really like it because … / What I really like about it is …*

♦ Everyone puts back their first item and has two minutes to choose one item they don't like. They get into different groups of four. This time they have to imagine that they do like it and tell the others why. The unpredictable task wakes them up a bit, but they usually need to say afterwards why *'Really, I don't like it'* (using 'really' to provide a contrast with the previous message), and then they can say why *'I really don't like it'* (ie I hate it), or why *'I don't really like it'* (ie I don't like it much, but I don't feel too strongly about it).

♦ Everyone puts back their second item and chooses another. They get into groups and explain why they like or don't like it. The others have to guess whether they're telling the truth or not.

Same/different

♦ Put out a lot of pictures. Students have one minute to pick one out at random. Ask them to get into pairs with the nearest person and compare their pictures. Afterwards ask them whether they were describing mostly similarities or differences. (One of the NLP 'metaprograms', which show how people tend to behave, is that some people tend to look for similarities between things, while some people concentrate first on differences.)

♦ Everyone picks a new picture at random. They mingle and try to find someone whose picture is similar in some way. As soon as they have found someone, they have to find six or more similarities. If there's nothing obvious – particularly for the final pairs to form, help them find sentences such as: *They're both pieces of paper. They're both rectangular. They both contain the colour blue …*

♦ Everyone chooses a new picture. They mingle and find someone whose picture is very similar, then they find as many differences as possible.

Revision

♦ Students choose two pictures which represent something they have learnt in class. The class forms two concentric circles, the inner circle facing out and the outer circle facing in, so students are in facing pairs. Students discuss their pictures and their learning with the person opposite for two minutes. The outer circle then moves one place to the right and the newly-formed pairs discuss their pictures. Move round three or four times.

Once you've started using your 'Pandora's box' of bits and pieces, you'll find lots of occasions when you think of activities which are relevant to your students. For example, a picture becomes the starting points for a story, a magazine article stimulates creative writing or descriptive writing. You can even set your students the task of using Pandora's box and creating and running language practice activities for other groups.

Mind Maps®

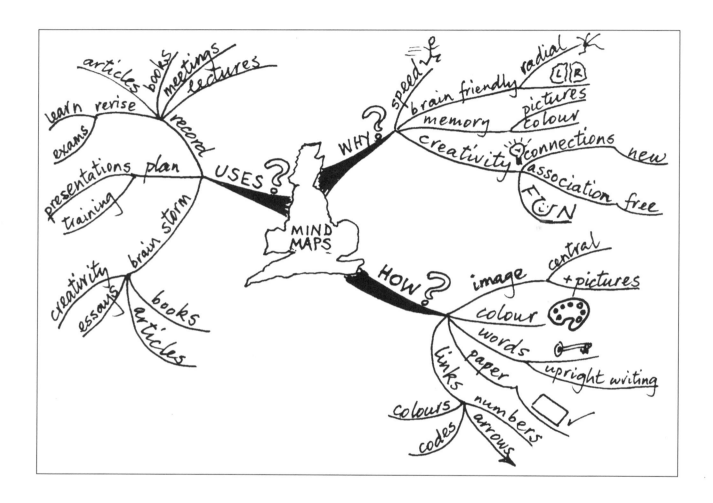

Mind Maps reflect the way the brain works best naturally – in a radial, branching fashion rather than a linear one – and this enables us to generate lots of ideas very quickly. Because they are highly visual, they are quick to do and easy to remember – and every one is different. Mind Maps are an excellent tool

- for brainstorming ideas to introduce a topic, make a presentation, do a project or write an essay
- as a substitute for a script or notes from which to speak when presenting, training or teaching
- for taking notes from talks
- to explain the general idea of something to people
- for summarising a book or recapping what's been covered in a lecture
- and many more …

Mind Maps are not specifically an NLP technique, but they exemplify many of the practical applications of NLP to teaching. They originated with Tony Buzan in a book he wrote in 1974 called '*Use your Head*'. In his second year at university, Buzan, overwhelmed with work, wanted to find answers to the question '*How can I use my brain most effectively to cope with all of this learning I have to do?*' but he failed to find any books to help him. So he himself began to explore this whole, huge area of learning, memorisation, creative thinking and so on - an exploration that he continues to this day.

So how can you and your students use Mind Maps in the context of teaching and learning English?

You can use them for brainstorming vocabulary ideas for lessons or in place of a lesson plan to have beside you during the lesson. You can give them to students (on the board or on the wall) at the beginning of a lesson, or the week or the term, to show them what they are going to be learning.

Teach your students to use Mind Maps too. For all the purposes outlined above, and for summarising their learning over the past lesson, week or term, or for planning their exam revision.

How to do it

Take a central idea, eg 'house', and write it in the middle of the Mind Map. Think of anything connected with the word 'house'. For a main idea (eg types of house, rooms in a house) start a main branch on a new line radiating out from the key word. Write supplementary ideas or examples on smaller lines coming off the main branches. You might start like this:

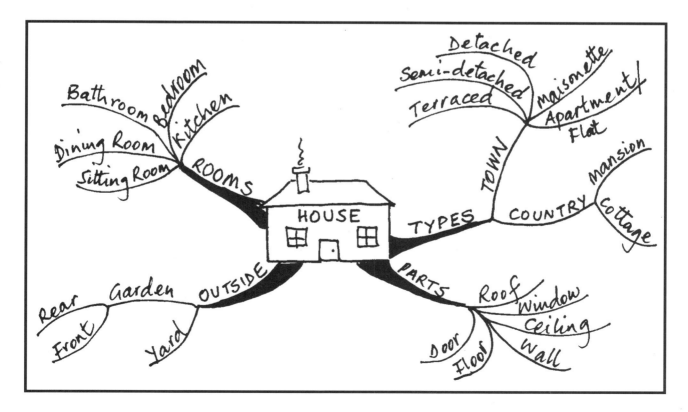

Ten laws of mindmapping

These 'laws' have sound reasons behind them, but you may feel inclined to break some of them once you get going and establish your own style.

- Use as large a sheet of paper as possible (A3 rather than A4 if you can)
- Have the paper horizontal rather than upright
- Always use a central image
- Use thicker lines for the major branches connected to the central image
- Write words on lines of the same length as the word
- Keep the writing as upright as possible
- Use only one key word per line
- Use lots of pictures, symbols and images
- Use lots of colours
- Link things using arrows, colours or codes

Show students some examples of Mind Maps (*The Mind Map Book* by Tony Buzan is a great source) and give them some simple ideas to work on.

When Jane's daughter, Tamsin, was 11 she produced the following Mind Map on the theme of 'Christmas'.

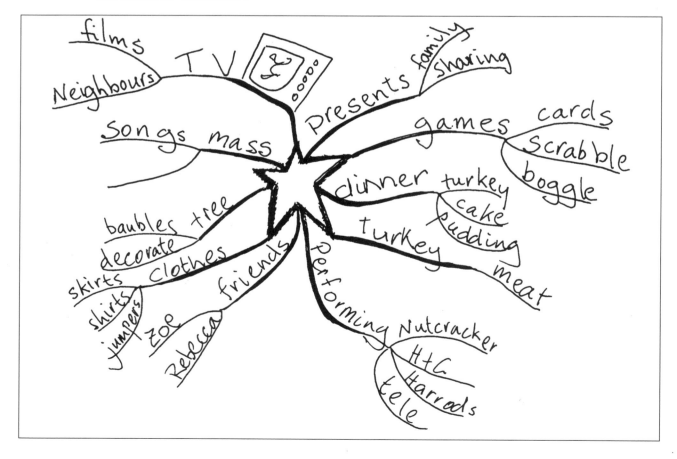

Tune up your auditory skills

I hear the drizzle of the rain, like a memory it falls
Soft and warm continuing, tapping on my roof and walls

Kathy's Song PAUL SIMON

Learning a language successfully has a lot to do with good auditory acuity ... good listening and sound discrimination skills. English language teachers tend to be pretty good at providing practice in this area. For years we've been using interesting cassettes with dialogues in a wide variety of accents, stories, songs, chants, music, pronunciation exercises, sound effects, games like Chinese Whispers, and so on. Some of us have been using drills too, frowned upon by many, but great for practising listening and speaking skills (especially when used creatively), and welcomed especially by learners who are highly auditory.

Learners with a strong auditory preference often like to repeat things in their own head after hearing them said. In order for this to happen, you need to pause frequently in your delivery. It may be that you already have this skill. When we first trained to become teachers (all those years ago) and learnt to make ourselves intelligible to foreign language learners, we were told not to slow down our delivery because that would distort it, but rather to pause after each sense group. We still offer (and take) this advice today.

Here are some suggestions to add to all the auditory things you're already doing in the classroom. Not all of them involve listening to language or even to verbal meaning or words. There are many other things one can listen out for as a way of enhancing auditory skills.

Listen and guess the appearance   Students listen to a story or song on cassette and try to describe the appearance of the speaker or singer from the sound of their voice. You then show them a picture and they say what they got correct and where there were differences.

Listen and describe   Students listen to a 'sound only' video sequence. (They can either shut their eyes, turn around or else you can cover the video with a jacket or coat.) As they listen, they imagine the picture: the characters, the setting and so on. Students share their descriptions and then watch the sequence with sound and vision to see how accurate they were.

Listen and repeat ... if it's true!   To make drills more interesting, make statements about a picture which you project on the OHP or which the students have in front of them. If what you say is true, the students repeat it verbatim. If it is false, the students say: *'That's not true'*. (You can also add a K element by getting them to put their right hand up if something is true, their left hand if it's false). An optional phase is correcting the false statements. Alternatively you can use the real world as your reference, eg

T *They speak French in Canada.*   SS *They speak French in Canada.*

T *They speak Dutch in Germany.*   SS *That's not true!*

Stand up and notice   Give each group of students a different secret word. The class then listens to a song or story where there is a lot of repetition of the secret words. Every time the group hears their particular word they stand up and sit down again. They must also notice when the other groups stand up to see if they can identify their words too. In the '*hospital story*', the four words are HOSPITAL, DOCTOR, NURSE and PATIENT.

A hospital story

Once upon a time there were two hospitals on opposite sides of the road. One was a very big hospital, where a lot of doctors and nurses worked, caring for a very large number of patients. The other was quite a small hospital, where a few nurses and even fewer doctors worked, caring for quite a small number of patients.

In the large hospital, the doctors had the most up-to-date expensive equipment and the nurses were all highly trained. In the small hospital, the doctors didn't have very much equipment at all, but the rooms were comfortable and nurses spent a lot of time talking to the patients, explaining what the doctors were doing, asking how the patients were feeling, and generally caring for them.

And guess what? The doctors and nurses in the large hospital were very surprised to notice that the patients in the small hospital seemed to get better much more quickly.

One of the doctors from the large hospital went into the small hospital and watched a nurse spend a lot of time with an elderly patient. When the nurse went away, the doctor went over to talk to the patient. He asked her what made this hospital so special. The old woman replied, 'Well, doctor, I think it's because the nurses are so patient!'

Listen for the instruments   Students listen to a piece of music either to spot a particular instrument or else to identify as many instruments as they can (*Peter and the Wolf* by Prokofiev is ideal for this.) Vocabulary can be pre-taught, or may emerge as a result of the task.

Echo listening   Teach students this technique to try at home. Each person listens to a tape of spoken language (preferably a monologue). As they listen they repeat what they hear as exactly as possible (sounds, timing, intonation, rhythm, etc) without stopping the tape. This means that they are about three seconds behind the tape, like an echo, producing what they have just heard, while listening to the next part. If they make a mistake, they go back to the beginning and start again. This is easier than it sounds and the concentration demanded by the overload of information can have a wonderful effect on students' pronunciation.

Breaking the visual/auditory link

Seeing and hearing   Have you noticed that when you introduce new vocabulary to students aurally their pronunciation is usually excellent, but the moment they see the words written down, they start pronouncing what they *see*? What they correctly pronounced *'Lunden'* becomes *'Lon-don'* and *'thought'* becomes *'thowt'* or worse! The eyes interfere with the ears.

One way of breaking this link is simply to point it out to students. Either write words in phonemic script, or as they are said, eg *'Lunden'* for *'London'*, *'Lester'* for *'Leicester'*, *'an don we go'* for *'and on we go'*, etc. You might like to point out that many UK teenagers write *'luv'* for *'love'* because that's the way it's said.

Write *'Leicester'* and *'Lester'* on the board and ask students what the difference in pronunciation is. The answer, of course, is that there is no difference. You may still have to work quite hard to get all the class saying the words exactly the same.

What is more interesting is that, particularly with older learners, the pronunciation problems occur before they've seen the word written down. You give them a clear model, but they say what they think the pronunciation should be, not what they actually hear. This is presumably because they are visualising the way the word is written and then pronouncing what they 'see' internally.

Again, the way to break the link is to explain to students what they are doing and then to help them make a double mental image – one is the way the word is spelt, and the other the way the word is pronounced.

Internal auditory monitoring   Another way to loosen the visual link is to put in an internal auditory phase before speaking. First students listen to a clear model. Then they 'replay' the sound of the model in their heads. Next they hear in their heads the sound of themselves saying the words in exactly the same way as they have just heard it. Finally they say the words aloud.

Listen to a story, song or text   You will already be using lots of interesting ideas for exploiting stories and songs. The ones here have been selected because they emphasise the auditory element and are to do first and foremost with careful listening.

- Stand up (or put up your hand) when you hear a specific word.
- Stand up (or put up your hand) when you hear a word beginning with or containing a specific letter.
- Find answers to 'signpost questions' (ie questions asked before the story is read).
- Listen out for words that are semantically or grammatically incorrect.
- Identify differences between what they hear and what is written down.

We are not suggesting that you only do this with a text. Some of these ideas make a good first listening activity, giving students a chance consciously to pay attention to a specific part of the text while being less consciously exposed to the rest of it, so that it will be easier for them the next time they hear it. We would expect to do a range of different activities with most texts.

Listen to the rhythm   Students listen to a very short dialogue or jazz chant and then repeat it without words, but retaining the rhythm and intonation of it: da di da di doo di da! Later, they put the words back in.

Sound discrimination   This is the classic 'ship/sheep' minimal pair type of activity. The teacher draws the two things on the board (or simply writes the two words), numbering them 1 and 2 and then says one of the pair of words. Students point to – or call out the number of – the one they think has been said. After some repetition, students can then test the teacher.

Follow instructions   Any situation in which students follow instructions practises their listening skills. One of the first things we teach at any level is all basic classroom instructions ('*open your books*', '*turn to page …*', '*get into pairs*', etc). At beginner and elementary level, as in the Total Physical Response method, we give instructions for students to do things in the classroom, eg '*touch the back wall*', '*pick up a blue book*', '*touch your nose*', etc. We indicate with nods, pointing, encouring looks, etc, which students are succeeding, and when someone has completed the task successfully. We do lots of recapping and repetition, and instructions get gradually more complicated. This is particularly effective with very young learners who are used to guessing because they don't understand things. In fact it is possible to be much less precise about grading 'teacher' language with young children than it is with adults who can often get frustrated if they don't fully understand.

MM, YES, NO, YOU, ME!

Purpose

To get students to experiment with and extend their tone of voice.

Language focus

Pronunciation.

PROCEDURE

- Ask students how many different meanings 'Mm' can have, and get them to demonstrate how to say it each time (eg 'Yes', 'No', 'Maybe', 'Stop!', 'Sorry?', 'Don't do that', 'I'm going to get you!' etc).

- Students work in pairs and have a conversation using only 'mm', which they must say in turn in as many different ways as they can think of.

- Students have a conversation using the words 'yes' and 'no' only. This could be done in pairs, or better still, as a mingle, where they all get up and walk around the classroom, talking to different people.

- They add the words 'you' and 'me' to their conversation, so they now have great possibilities with mm, yes, no, you and me.

- Have some students act out some of their conversations.

- Discuss the importance of intonation and tone of voice for communication.

Taking account of students' need for ...
AUDITORY input

Cassettes   Inner voice   Rhyme   Roleplay

Video   Acting out   Music   Oral pairwork

Rhythm   Choral speaking   Speaking slowly

Songs   Video   Listen and repeat

Repetition   Pronunciation   Discussion   Echo listening

Dictation   Silence   The sound of words   Clapping

Sound effects   Raps   Speaking aloud

Background music

Reading aloud   Chinese whispers   Chants

Guided fantasies   Listening to stories

Speak loudly or quietly   Everyone speaking together   Different tones of voice

Add your own ideas to this page.

Yes, but ...

I haven't got access to a photocopier. I can't give out lots of extra pieces of paper to each student every lesson.

Yes, and ...

- Use dialogues, pictures, etc, from your coursebook for the language content.
- Dictate the text, teacher to all students, or as a communicative dictation: Give a different part of the text to one person in each group – that person dictates the text to the others – students form new groups consisting of one member from each of the original groups – each person dictates their own part of the text to the others in the group so that everyone has a copy of the complete text – you display a complete copy of the text on the board, on a poster, or on a sheet of paper on the wall so that everyone checks their own version.
- Prepare large posters of the material and stick them around the walls. Wallpaper remnants are a cheap source of large rolls of paper. Enlist the help of student volunteers who want extra language practice. Keep the posters for future use.
- Stick one small copy of the text on the wall (or on a notice board to which they have access). Every student copies it before the next lesson without making a single mistake. Students check each others' accuracy.

Music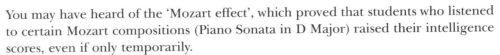

You may have heard of the 'Mozart effect', which proved that students who listened to certain Mozart compositions (Piano Sonata in D Major) raised their intelligence scores, even if only temporarily.

Music has a powerful effect on the body, mind and emotions which is not yet fully understood. (Why do so many of us have similar responses – like the shiver down the spine – at particular points in certain pieces of music?) What is clear is that music can be used to enhance learning. It activates emotions and long-term memory and fully engages the brain's most receptive states. Which music is best for learning? The research seems to say – perhaps as one would expect – that it depends on the individual and on what you are trying to achieve.

Different music is good for different occasions and for achieving different outcomes. You do not need to confine yourself to classical music. Finding out what your students listen to and playing one of their favourites can give them a positive surprise at the beginning of a lesson. Since they are all likely to have different tastes, you might also get students to take turns in providing the introductory music. Don't assume that students will only choose pop music. When Susan was playing Mozart as background music in class, some of the students asked if they could change it – and replaced it with Beethoven.

Try some of the following ways of incorporating music into your teaching. We have recommended specific examples of certain types of music for different activities, but don't worry if you can't find these exact selections. Take risks, experiment, have fun, and see and hear what you get! If it works, use it again. If it doesn't, don't. Remember that there may be cultural differences in the way different sorts of music are perceived. You and your students will know what works for you.

 Setting the mood   Have music playing as students come into the classroom. Choose the music according the mood you would like to induce in the students – or that you want to match. If you think they're going to be a bit sluggish after lunch, you might start with something relaxing (to 'pace' their current mood) – and then play something more lively to wake them up (and 'lead' them to the state you want them in for learning). Well-known classical selections are good welcomers.

 Energisers   Dramatic or lively music (try Latin American or African rhythms) can be an energiser, particularly if played during a stretch break between activities.

 Dance   Try starting with dance music and teaching a simple dance as an energiser to get everyone working together. We've been successful (even with teenagers) with American line dances, circle dances, English and Scottish country dances, and the waltz. Teach basic vocabulary such as *step, tap, turn*, etc, and then encourage students who know the dances – or who pick them up quickly – each to teach a small group before the class dances together. Try putting simple words to action dances, eg for the *Macarena*, students came up with:

> *Arm, arm; palm, palm; elbow, elbow; ear, ear*
> *Chest, chest, hip, hip; Ooh, Macarena – clap.*

Signal a change   Change the mood of a lesson or introduce a new theme by playing a short extract of appropriate music. Either play it in the background while students are getting out books, moving furniture or getting into groups, or ask students to relax, take a break and listen.

Introduce a theme   Play music according to the theme of the lesson, either as students walk into the classroom, or by specifically asking them to listen and guess what the lesson is going to be about. Popular movie theme tunes can be particularly useful.

Language generators   Play different selections of music – jazz, romantic, discordant modern classical, gentle harmonious classical, nursery rhymes, Latin American, something dramatic such as Saint Saëns' *Danse Macabre*, etc. Ask students to respond after each piece. They might say what they do or don't like, grading the pieces in order of preference. Ask them to visualise a picture as they listen and then describe their pictures. Students describe the music in terms of each of the other senses. Or they listen quietly to a piece of music and then brainstorm all the adjectives to describe the feelings it inspired in them (you can then use this as classroom research into which pieces of music to use with the class to inspire particular moods). Students can also write a description, or a list of emotions, or their word picture for each piece – these are then jumbled, the pieces are played again and other students try to match the writing with the music. All of this can lead to class discussion of types of music, the effect music has on us, and how we might use music in class to aid learning.

Background music   Play music in the background when students are reading quietly, doing tests, or working in pairs or groups or on project work. Classical music by Haydn, Mozart, Beethoven or Bach usually provides the right balance of stimulation and relaxation, without being too distracting if people are trying to concentrate. We don't recommend songs with words as background music when students need to concentrate on other language work. However, playing songs quietly in the background can be an excellent way of building up students' non-conscious awareness of language when it is not likely to interfere with other work.

Relaxation, guided fantasy   Play gentle background music for relaxation exercises and guided fantasy. 'New Age' pieces (by composers such as Kitaro or Tim Wheater) are particularly good for relaxation because they don't have specific tunes to latch on to, and they encourage a feeling of 'floating' from one thought to another. We recommend not using music which is very well-known because people will probably have acquired emotional links which may interefere with their relaxation.

Going out with a bang   Put on inspiring 'feel-good' music as students are gathering up their books and leaving the classroom. Send them out with smiles on their faces! (Try *'Wonderful world'*, *'Time of my life'*, *'Simply the best'*, etc.)

Silence   Don't overdo the music. Not everyone likes it all the time, and not everyone likes the same sort of music. Silence is good too.

HINT Before you switch off a CD or cassette you have been playing, turn it down gradually so that you don't destroy the mood you have just created. It can be effective to 'fade it in' too.

41

Recommended music

Classical dramatic Beethoven *Fifth Symphony*; Beethoven *Ninth Symphony*, the *Ode to Joy* (end of last movement); Handel *The Messiah*, the *Hallelujah Chorus*; Richard Strauss *Also sprach Zarathustra* (the opening – used as the theme music for the film *2001*); Verdi *Requiem*, the *Dies Irae*; Wagner *Tannhauser*; Yanni *In the Mirror*; Strauss *Blue Danube Waltz*; Karl Orff *Carmina Burana*; Mozart *Requiem*.

Classical relaxing Bach's Violin Concertos (especially the double concerto); Beethoven *Moonlight Sonata*; Brahms *Violin Concerto in D*; Mozart *Elvira Madigan*; Pachelbel *Canon*; Smetana *Ma Vlast* (opening sequence); Vivaldi *Four Seasons*; Górecki *Symphony Nº 3*; Satie *Trois Gymnopédies*.

Movie soundtracks *Chariots of Fire, Close Encounters, Star Wars, The Mission, Jaws, Working Girl, Titanic, Death in Venice* (Mahler's *Fifth Symphony*, fourth movement), *Brief Encounter* (Rachmaninov *Piano Concerto Nº 2 in C minor*).

Nowadays the effect of music is well recognised and specific selections of particular types of music are available. Look in your record store for 'music for relaxation', 'romantic music', 'Baroque music' (particularly recommended for inducing a relaxed learning state), Gregorian chants, Elizabethan music, pan pipes, Indian sitar music, New Age music, Gaelic or Celtic music by Enya, the Chieftains or Clannad, etc. Then go through your collection and use music you like! Jazz, maybe?

Yes, but... Yes, and...

I totally believe in using NLP in the classroom, but how do I deal with resistance from my students?

- Are you sure you're not just making an excuse for not trying out new ideas? Have you actually tried some of these ideas with students, or have you just assumed that they won't like them? Choose one activity you think they would like. Do it.

- Explain to the students what you are doing and why. Ask them for their help to make the activities work. Try it together. Afterwards, discuss with them how the activity worked and how we could all do it better next time.

- Ask yourself (and the students) why they don't want to do the activities.

- Are they shy or embarrassed? Make it into a game. The game of learning English. Promote a classroom atmosphere where 'mistakes' become 'feedback'.

- Do they think it's not serious enough? Explain that research shows that people learn more quickly and easily when they are relaxed and having fun, when they are interacting and using the language. (Think how easily young children learn.) Do 'serious' activities too, and set 'serious' homework for those who want it.

- You know your students. Think of three things you could do to encourage them to try some activities. And three things to help your students learn more easily.

- Have in mind a particular group of students you think you couldn't use these activities with. Open *Handing Over* at random. Find one thing on the page that you could do with the students. Then find one thing that you couldn't do – and suggest three different ways of doing it. (The second activity will probably have most impact on your relationship with the students and on their learning.)

- One element of good teaching is variety. It isn't a question of all or nothing: incorporate NLP techniques into what you're already doing, as appropriate.

Moving into the kinaesthetic

A turtle makes progress when it sticks its neck out!

<small>ANON</small>

Although most of us have probably incorporated some kinaesthetic elements into our teaching, we feel (!) that this is almost certainly the area that we exploit least, unless we are involved in teaching young learners. Yes, we use realia whenever we can and whenever it's appropriate, especially at beginner level, so that students can hold or touch the things that they're learning the names of. And yes, we often use mime to convey meaning, and sometimes we get students to use it too or to act things out. But we could do a whole lot more – with all age groups and class levels. This is not just a question of creating a balance with visual and auditory activities, so as to satisfy all learner preferences and provide multi-sensory teaching. There is increasing evidence that memory is enhanced by movement (think of actors pacing up and down as they learn their lines), and that everyone can benefit from moving around as they learn. It's also very much to do with helping learners get into and maintain an optimal learning state.

One of the NLP presuppositions states that mind and body are inter-connected: they are part of the same system. Recent research into the brain shows that if we sit still and concentrate on something for long, we begin to wind down physically and mentally. Eric Jensen suggests that different age groups may have different concentration span thresholds: 5 to 10 minutes for young learners, 10 to 15 minutes for adolescents, and 15 to 25 minutes for adults. In order to recharge our physical and mental batteries, we need to activate our body to boost our circulation. This gets more blood flowing around and carrying oxygen to refuel different parts of our body, including – most importantly in terms of learning – our brain.

Another very compelling argument for incorporating more 'K' into our teaching is to be found in the research connected with educational kinesiology (also known as Brain Gym). This is based on research which shows that by making certain physical movements, particularly ones which involve using opposite arms and legs (as when we march), we forge pathways in our brain, either creating new connections or radically improving old ones that may have been working less well through lack of use. These types of exercise can really maximise our students' learning power, and, of course, they can maximise our own learning power too.

The word kinaesthetic refers to movement (psychomotor), to touch and sensation (tactile), and also to emotion (visceral). Emotion is covered in a separate section (see page 51), so here we concentrate on movement, touch and sensation. Having said that, many of the activities have a strong emotional component too: they have a tendency to get people excited and involved. They often make them laugh as well. Laughter is a terrifically powerful force. Not only does it relax us and make us more alert and open to learning, it also helps us remember better and – through increasing the white blood corpuscle count – keeps us healthier.

Tactile activities

Many kinaesthetic learners need to move to help their thinking processes. This is well known in societies where people regularly carry 'worry beads' and the like. Nowadays it is possible to find 'stress' balls (malleable balls which you 'knead'), Chinese chiming balls (which you work in pairs in one hand), kooshes (colourful soft plastic balls with lots of 'tentacles', a bit like baby hedgehogs), 'meditation bangles' (which you turn inside out and round about), as well as worry beads. Many students will appreciate being allowed to bring their own such 'toys' to manipulate in class – or being allowed to use a selection of yours. Doodling might also be allowed, as long as it doesn't actually become the main focus of attention!

Any activity where students use realia or props is by definition tactile. So too is any activity using artistic materials, especially things like plasticine or lego. Cuisenaire rods are tactile. Cards are tactile. Games with dice and counters are tactile. So is project work or any activity where students are involved in making things or brainstorming ideas onto flipchart paper and so on. Here are a few more ideas.

Feel and describe   Create a 'feely bag'. Students take it in turns to put their hand into the bag and take hold of one of the objects inside, feeling it carefully to guess what it is, but unable to see it. The other students ask yes/no questions to get clues so they can guess what the object is. Possible contents: rubber, paper clip, sponge, tissue, bow tie, baby's dummy, orange, computer disk, cotton reel, key, cassette, film canister, rubber band, artificial flower, teaspoon, ring, earring, brooch, necklace, credit card, sweets, etc.

Blind man's buff   One student is blindfolded and the others form a circle. The blindfolded person is turned around a few times to disorient them and then they try to touch someone in the circle. By feeling the person's face and hair, they must guess who it is, while describing what they can feel (eg It's a girl, she's got long hair, she's wearing glasses, etc). If they guess the name correctly, that person goes into the centre. (This is a traditional English children's game.)

Create with a pipe cleaner   Demonstrate first yourself. Take some plasticine or a pipe cleaner (woolly-covered wire about 15 cms long, used for cleaning a smoker's pipe) and bend or mould it to represent something (eg a telephone, a dog, a chair, etc). Ask students to guess what it is. Give one to each student and have them create their own objects – which can be as fanciful as they like. Students can work in groups, or show their objects to the whole class.

Construct it   Each group of students has a few pieces of lego (or Cuisenaire rods or children's building toys) and a picture of what they are to construct. Once they have constructed the object, they write instructions for another group to make the same object. They then take the object apart and pass the instructions to the next group who try to reconstruct the object without the benefit of the picture. Afterwards groups discuss which was easier, and why.

Psychomotor activities

We divide psychomotor activities into two groups:

♦ activities which can serve as short physical 'energisers' to enhance the learning process as previously described. They are not language-learning activities in their own right (although they often have a listening comprehension component involving careful following of instructions). Their main function is to serve rather as 'punctuators', providing a quick change of activity and a rest and a recharge for the brain. Breathing exercises, physical exercises, Brain Gym and dancing would fall into this category.

♦ language-learning activities proper which have a strong psychomotor element. These would include such things as roleplay, mime, games like 'Simon says' and so on, many of which you are probably already using.

Quick energisers

The simplest energiser is to stand up! If you notice students are getting lethargic, ask them to stand up, tell them why, and carry on teaching like that for a few minutes. Better still, get them to stand up before they get to the lethargic stage – especially if it is done as part of a normal activity, eg ask them to change partners, groups or seats, or get them to come up to the board to write, or use mingles, etc. If students need more of a boost, add one of these simple energisers. They can be done sitting down, but are more beneficial if done standing up. The language focus is following instructions, imperatives, parts of the body, and verbs of movement.

Deep abdominal breathing   Breathe in through your nose, taking the breath right down to your stomach so that your stomach moves out (rather than your chest and shoulders), then breathe out through your mouth, bringing your stomach back in as you do so. Think 'down'. Do this three or four times.

Tell people in advance that they might get a bit dizzy from the unaccustomed extra oxygen. If they do, all they need to do is sit down and breathe normally.

Stretch   your arms above your head. Really stretch. Link your thumbs together and stretch higher. And yawn. A really big yawn.

Raise your shoulders   to your ears, then drop them – shoulders, not ears!

Circle your arms   together backwards four times, then forwards four times. Then rotate alternate arms backwards four times (like doing the backstroke), then forwards four times (like doing the crawl). Then circle one arm forwards and the other backwards – and then do the same with arms going the other way.

WARNING

Check carefully if you're working in a cultural environment which is not your own, or with students from a variety of different cultures, that there are no cultural problems connected with activities which involve students touching each other in any way.

Check whether any students in the group have physical problems which mean they should avoid doing particular physical exercises or breathing activities. Always encourage students (by telling and demonstrating) to start movements gently and then to do them more strongly if appropriate.

Drop your chin to your chest   To relieve tension in your neck, very slowly look down, then bring your head up again. Keeping your chin parallel with the floor, look round to the right as far as possible, then back to the centre. Look round to the left – and back to the centre. Very slowly and carefully lift your chin and look up to the ceiling, and then back to the centre. You can also synchronise this sequence with deep breathing – breathe in as you look in the different directions and breathe out as you come back to the centre.

Clench your fists   then open your hands and stretch your fingers really wide. Do this slowly four times, then double speed eight times.

Shake your hands   shake your arms, shake your shoulders, shake your head, shake your legs, shake your feet, shake your lips, shake your ears, shake … anything else you can think of!

Loosen up your face   Make facial grimaces … as exaggerated as possible. Exercise your jaw muscles (taking great care not to jerk anything), and your lip muscles, and screw up and relax your eyes. Put your lower lip over your upper lip and smile. Apart from being very silly and tending to make people laugh, this increases facial flexibility, and improves voice quality, projection and facial expressiveness. It also tones up facial muscles and helps us look youthful!

Teachers in Brazil doing the cross crawl with Susan Norman

Right hand to left knee   Bring up your left leg and – depending on how flexible you are – touch your left knee (or ankle) with your right hand (or elbow). Repeat slowly, left to right, right to left. This is the '*cross crawl*' from Brain Gym, which enhances the connections between the two hemispheres of the brain.

Marching on the spot   or round the room, swinging the opposite arm and leg together. This has a similar effect to the cross crawl above. Cross country skiers use this same movement to increase their stamina, and armies can go much farther at a regular march, rather than strolling.

Dancing   Put on some boppy music and get students up and moving around for a moment. We always allow them not to dance if they really don't want to, but tell them that they must at least move around the room rather than stay rooted to the spot. If you want to incorporate dancing in a slightly bigger way into your teaching or training, 'circle dancing' and 'line dancing' are both excellent as they are relatively simple to do and include everyone.

Tiger growl   Take a quick breath in as you bring your hands up, fingers curled downwards like claws; pause slightly, then bring your claws down sharply and let out a growl, bending your knees as you do so. Do this a couple of times.

Doing the gorilla thump on an NLP Diploma course with Jane Revell.

Gorilla thump   Thump your chest like a gorilla and say a deep long 'Ah' at the same time. A splendid energy raiser.

Language generators

Write your name in the air   as large as possible with your right hand, your left hand, with both hands, with your right leg, your left leg, with your nose, with your bottom! This is one of our favourite energisers – especially the last one! It can be adapted to words other than names: it's a good way of revising vocabulary, and can also be used to write whole sentences and positive affirmations, such as 'My English is excellent!' … complete with exclamation mark of course.

Stop the music   and mime a word or phrase that someone calls out. Or give them a question word which they must use to ask a question of the person next to them. Or play hand to nose (see next activity). Or stay perfectly still in the position you happen to be in. Or call out a word beginning with a particular letter, etc.

Hand to nose   When the music stops, the teacher calls out two parts of the body, eg 'hand to nose'. Each student puts one hand – gently – on the nearest person's nose. Pairs of words can get gradually more challenging, eg thumb to shoulder, little finger to ear, back to back, elbow to knee, hip to hip, wrist to toe, etc.

Mime revision   Students revise vocabulary by miming recently-learnt words for their partner to guess.

Touch something   blue, beginning with 't', made of wood, square, etc.

This is my nose   Students work in pairs. One points to their nose and says *'This is my nose'*. Their partner copies them and repeats the words. They then take turns in being the leader. If the leader tells the truth – eg when pointing to ears says, *'These are my ears'* – the partner copies and repeats the sentence. If however the leader lies – eg while pointing to eyes says, *'These are my ears'* – the partner corrects them either by repeating the same words but pointing to the correct part of the body, or by pointing to the same part of the body and saying the correct words.

Body magic   Students show one another strange things they can do with their bodies, eg rub your stomach while patting your head, roll your tongue, wiggle your ears, touch your nose with your tongue, etc, and ask, *'Can you do this?'* Others try to do it and demonstrate, saying *'Yes I can'* or *'No I can't'*.

Action songs, chants and raps   Children's songs like *'One finger, one thumb'* and *'Head, shoulders, knees and toes'* are great energisers too, as are chants and raps with added movements. Ask your students (in small groups) to make them up, using new vocabulary and structures and teach them to the rest of the class. Remember to join in too!

'My Bonnie lies over the ocean' can be turned into a great action song by getting students to stand up or sit down for every word beginning with a letter 'b'. Many other songs can be adapted in different ways too.

Clap stress   Teacher and students clap word stress or sentence rhythm, and/or stand on tiptoe for each stressed syllable or word, and/or students 'conduct' (like orchestra conductors) the rhythm and intonation of a sentence or a text, and/or they stand up for questions which rise at the end (eg many yes/no questions) and sit down for statements or questions (eg many wh-questions) which go down at the end.

Comment

Many teachers feel self-conscious or slightly silly about using these kinds of activity in the classroom. All we can say is that it took us some time to get round to doing it too, for the same kinds of reasons. Looking back, we're only sorry we didn't do it sooner! Over the last few years we have used these energisers with many different groups of people: young children, teenagers, adult language learners, teachers, even people in companies learning presentation skills. We know that they really do make a big difference to the learners' state of body and mind, and all the groups with whom we use them very quickly get to demand them if we occasionally forget.

PARTY MESSAGES

Purpose
To practise getting a message across using mime; fun.

Language focus
Any.

PROCEDURE

- Copy (or photocopy) the messages on the next page (or your own versions) and cut them up to have one message on each small piece of paper.

- Give each student a message, which they keep hidden.

- Students stand on the opposite side of the room from their partner and imagine that they are at a crowded, noisy party. Each person must get their message across to their partner within one minute by miming.

- When you call time, students come together to check if their interpretation coincides with the original message. It's more demanding and better language practice if they have to guess the exact words on the card.

- You can continue the activity by giving people additional messages.

Party Messages

I've got three brothers.	I've just been stung by a wasp. What can I put on it?
How many sisters have you got?	How about going to the zoo?
What's your mother's name?	You've spilt some soup on your trousers.
How old is your grandfather?	Did you borrow my French cookery book?
What does your father do?	Let's have dinner at the Mexican restaurant.
My friend comes from Spain.	Can I borrow your Spanish dictionary?
This is my uncle.	Have you got time for a game of ping pong later?
I live in north London.	Did you get to your tango class on time?
Where do you live?	Are you coming to our barbecue on Sunday?
What's your name?	See you at the concert next week.
Where's the red book?	There's a programme on Scottish dancing on TV tonight.
What colour is the door?	Do you want to go swimming tomorrow?
How do you do.	I've just cut my finger on the bread knife.
How are you?	Have you got a guide book on Brazil?
Give me that book please.	Did you remember to buy some teabags?
Where do you come from?	Can I borrow your book on impressionist painting?
The table is in the garden.	I'll see you outside the hairdresser's.
The cat is under the table.	Did you turn off the oven?
The dog is on the chair.	Shall we go to the ballet?
Where is the teacher?	Can you give me a lift home?
My grandmother is 76.	You've got a ladder in your tights.
My sister is 12.	I've got to be home before midnight.
I'm not Australian.	Let's eat at the Greek restaurant.
She's very angry.	Your trousers have split – here.
My book is green.	I'll meet you at the bus station at 9am.
My sister's got blue eyes.	There's a white stain on your sweater ... under your left arm.
My brother's got black hair.	Fancy going to the disco?
Have you got any dogs or cats?	Can I borrow your cassette recorder?
What's the teacher's name?	You've got some egg on your tie.
We've got three bedrooms in our house.	My baby sister's not very well.

Taking account of students' need for ...

KINAESTHETIC input

Mime   Simon says   Games   Roleplay

Rhythm   Engaging feelings   Relaxation

Questionnaires   Surveys   Mingling activities

Writing

Brain Gym   Real objects   Sitting in different groups, pairs

Physical exercise

Drawing

Acting out   Video   Taking notes

Activity stories

Warm ups   Songs

Practical project work   Moving around while learning

Expressing emotions   Touching

Add your own ideas to this page.

Yes, but ...	Yes, and ...
I don't want to discuss my feelings. Nor do my students.	Never demand or expect students to reveal their innermost thoughts and feelings. Introduce 'feeling' words gently with a series of activities. Make sure a safe atmosphere develops in the class and allow individuals to opt out if they wish. • Practise feeling words as vocabulary items. • Match feeling words to the times when other people might feel those feelings. • Complete specific feeling sentences, eg *I felt happy when …* *I felt angry when …* Students will not reveal more than they want to. Some will say or write about important moments in their lives, others will be more restrained. Accept any level of self-revelation. Concentrate on the language aspect, but be sure to acknowledge and respect greater depths of expression, and where appropriate respond to the emotion rather than the language. Express your own feelings gently too. Expressing yourself as a human being rather than as a teacher will help build your relationship with students. However, the key is **appropriacy**. Make sure that the feelings you express are appropriate to the situation and to the age and emotional maturity of your students. But if you don't express your feelings, why should students? You set the tone.

Engaging the emotions

Triune brain theory shows that we have three 'brains'. The reptilian brain at the base of the skull is most concerned with our physical well-being and our 'fight or flight' response. The mammalian brain is concerned with the emotions, and our cerebral cortex, the thinking brain, is concerned with 'higher' intellectual functions. As in Abraham Maslow's theory, our basic needs must be met before we can give our attention to higher thinking skills. Our most immediate physical safety and comfort needs are met in most teaching circumstances – although we all know how difficult it can be to keep students on task when it is too hot or too cold, or everyone is beginning to think about lunch. It is relatively easy to take account of such factors. More difficult, because it is more personal and individual, is to take account of people's emotional needs, and yet unless we do, students' learning is bound to be impaired.

The environment in which people learn is obviously crucially important and yet most schools still seem to have been designed to impede learning, not enhance it. Working within the obvious limitations, try to make classrooms and training rooms as comfortable, welcoming and pleasant as possible. Simply making sure students get natural light, fresh air and plenty of water to drink will improve most people's learning, and it's amazing what effect you can have just with a few flowers, some music, pictures and posters on the wall, and a couple of large, brightly-coloured sheets or throws over main display tables (which also gives you some covered storage area for clearing mess too).

understanding

self-fulfilment

love, feeling of belonging

competence, prestige and esteem

security and safety

physiological needs: food, shelter, warmth, etc

Abraham Maslow's 'Hierarchy of Needs'

Maslow's triangle shows how people are motivated. The needs at the base of the triangle must be satisfied first. For example, if your body is uncomfortable, you can't think clearly. If your safety is threatened, you won't be interested in learning.

One simple way to take the emotional temperature of the class is to give people the chance to say how they are feeling. This means teaching words to express feelings and using them in different ways on a regular basis. It is quite important to build up the sort of atmosphere where people feel confident to express feelings openly and to encourage students to respect the feelings of others. This can be quite a gradual process. When in doubt, concentrate on the language aspect and talk about the feelings of others, or how other people might be feeling in certain circumstances. People do not express more than they want to, but sometimes a teacher can set up quite heavy pressure to express intimate feelings, just by setting up a particular exercise that other people in the class are willing to go along with. Always offer people the option of keeping their feelings private, or ask them to choose an experience or an emotion that they are happy to share with others. Try some of the activities on the next pages.

⧫ Students mime how they are feeling to a partner. When everyone has guessed, on the count of three, everyone shouts out the adjective to describe their partner.

⧫ Everyone thinks of a sentence to describe how they are feeling. Everyone says it aloud at the same time. Calling out is quite energising and allows people to say whatever they want, without the embarrassment of other people hearing.

⧫ Take five or ten minutes occasionally for people to give an adjective to say how they're feeling, or to share something important that's happened to them.

⧫ With new or young classes, people choose an adjective starting with the first letter of their name (eg Serene Susan, Generous Ginny). They mingle and introduce themselves, and others greet them, using the adjective and their name.

⧫ As an energiser, ask people to walk round the room showing with their bodies whichever adjective you call out, eg *happy, bored, miserable, tired, excited, angry, hungry, intelligent, romantic, weak, nervous, worried, frightened, sleepy, enthusiastic.* End with a positive, upbeat emotion.

⧫ Sing a very repetitive song, such as *Ten Green Bottles*, or *99 Bottles of Beer on the Wall*, and call out a different adjective to describe the way in which the next verse can be sung, eg *happy, slow, exhausted, joyful*, etc.

⧫ The class stands in a circle. You start by saying an adjective, eg *happy*, then mime that adjective, while pointing to someone and calling out a different adjective, eg *tired*. The person you are pointing at mimes the previous adjective (*happy*) and the people on either side of them mime the word you are saying (*tired*). The person you are pointing at then points at someone else, mimes the adjective you have just said (*tired*) and calls out a new adjective (eg *angry*) ... and so on.

⧫ Write on the board a list of adjectives which can easily be mimed. Students practise newly-learned items of vocabulary, phrases or structures, by moving round the room and saying them to one another in the manner of one of the words on the board. Their partner identifies the emotion and responds by saying something like: *You seem very excited. You said that very happily.*

Brainstormed emotions

⧫ Brainstorm words to describe emotions. Write them randomly on the board. Alternatively, prepare an OHP, or use the adjectives on pages 53-54. Sorting through information is an effective and relatively painless way of helping people learn it. Ask them to identify (by calling out, writing down or highlighting):
  • opposites and similes (eg *'the opposite of boring'*, or *'any opposites you can find'*)
  • words of three (or four or two) syllables
  • words which match a particular stress pattern (eg *conceited* oOo)
  • words beginning with each letter of the alphabet in order (everyone calls out)
  • words ending with different letters of the alphabet (you call out the letters)
  • words which can either end -*ed* or -*ing* (eg *excited/exciting*)
  • positive emotions (there may be some differences of opinion)
  • words describing a temporary state, eg *'tired'*, rather than words which might describe someone's personality, eg *'optimistic'* (hopefully there will be a lot of differences of opinion – see page 139 on 'loosening labels')
  • words they already know and which they could use with confidence
  • words containing particular sounds (eg 'k' – *sarcastic, obnoxious*)
  • words which can make anagrams of one another (eg *vile, evil*)

dull courageous joyful exciting cheerful
tiring depressed kind lovable furious gallant
miserable clever powerful
fascinating
warm friendly boring weary romantic
amiable
gentle
sincere refined virtuous uptight
uncompromising wistful well-behaved
handsome
vivacious
malicious sarcastic
good-natured curious impatient
quick-witted calm worried zealous afraid
scared
gay confident domineering
insincere obnoxious
eager generous disappointed
hateful vicious irascible
keen conceited serene reserved
adorable gracious unpretentious
angry unhappy wily
moody lucky old
cold demonstrative beautiful
lively passionate hot-headed
hard-headed interesting good mature
pessimistic impulsive
excitable jolly smug truthful
deceitful
civil crazy naughty
loving uncertain whimsical
slow frightening
brave mischievous evil nervous

sinister
sensitive
jovial
modest
nice
lonely
obsequious
insensitive
repulsive
querulous
affected
neat
attractive
sensible
seductive
tactful
responsible
caring
immature
blue
charming
tolerant
impulsive
sad
devoted
honest
alone
trustworthy
alert
uncomplaining
cross
well
thoughtful
hasty
touchy
ungrateful
unobtrusive
courteous
tired
urbane
witty
wild
unassuming
loyal
impertinent
cynical
quiet
yellow
civilised
hungry
elegant
sweet
hospitable
diligent
huffy
frightened
young
bold
bright
considerate
happy
lovely
untrustworthy
intelligent
ugly
vile
jealous
hard-working
wise
fearful
patient
bored
cowardly
hard
exhausted
vain
vulnerable
dynamic
mean
excited
vital
mad
wonderful
chivalrous
wary
queasy
intolerant
angelic
open
self-confident
polite
bad-tempered
optimistic
weak
nasty

♦ Choose 10 words to complete each of these sentences:

I would like to be more …   *I would like to be less …*

♦ Look up in a dictionary 10 words you didn't know. Translate them.

♦ Say each word in a way which expresses its meaning.

♦ Choose 10 words to draw in a way which expresses their meaning.

♦ Choose 10 words to complete each of these sentences:

People often feel … when …   *I felt … when …*

♦ Choose three words you like the look of, three you like the sound of, three you like the feel of, and three whose meaning you like.

Gift cards

♦ Photocopy the 'gift' cards on pages 56-57 several times onto different coloured pieces of paper, cut them up and try many of the activities related to the brainstormed words above, as well as some of the following – and you can probably think of many more.

• Mix up the words into a basket and offer them to each person as they enter or leave the classroom, simply to take as a gift.

• Each person takes a word and tries to find someone who has a word with the similar or opposite meaning.

• Students each take a word at random and discuss with their partner whether the colour it is printed on is appropriate to the meaning.

• Choose 15 or 20 of the words which are most useful to your students. Each small group is given two sets of the same words. They lay them face down on the table and play 'pelmanism': in turn they turn over two cards. If the cards contain the same word, the student defines the word and uses it in a sentence which the other students agree is appropriate; they take the two cards and have another go. The winner is the person who collects the most pairs of cards.

• Give several words to each group of students. From these they choose one each and draw a 'word spider' (a sort of mini Mind Map – see page 32). They write words such as the related parts of speech (noun, verb, adjective, adverb), opposites, similar meanings, sample sentences, the word stress, etc.

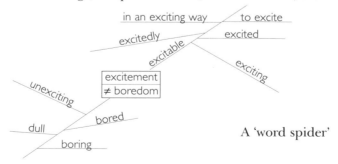

A 'word spider'

• Students sit quietly and think of a problem or current situation with which they would like some help; they then take a word from the basket and consider what insight this gives them into the situation. Discuss with a partner if appropriate.

ABUNDANCE	ADVENTURE	ASSISTANCE	AUTHORITY	AUTONOMY
AWE	BALANCE	BALM	BEAUTY	BELIEF
BRIGHTNESS	CALMNESS	CAUTION	CERTAINTY	CHALLENGE
CHEERFULNESS	CLARITY	COMFORT	COMMUNICATION	COMPASSION
CONCENTRATION	CONFIDENCE	CONTENTMENT	COURAGE	CREATIVITY
DECISIVENESS	DELIGHT	DIGNITY	DILIGENCE	EFFICIENCY
ELEGANCE	ENDURANCE	ENERGY	ENTHUSIASM	EXCELLENCE
EXCITEMENT	EXUBERANCE	FAIRNESS	FAITH	FLEXIBILITY
FORGIVENESS	FREEDOM	FRIENDSHIP	FUN	GENEROSITY
GENTLENESS	GRACE	GRATITUDE	GROWTH	HAPPINESS
HARMONY	HEALING	HEALTH	HONESTY	HONOUR
HOPE	HUMILITY	HUMOUR	INDEPENDENCE	INNOVATION

INSPIRATION	INTEGRITY	INTELLIGENCE	JOY	JUSTICE
KINDNESS	KNOWLEDGE	LAUGHTER	LEARNING	LEISURE
LIFE	LIGHT	LIGHTNESS	LIVELINESS	LOVE
MAGIC	MASTERY	OBEDIENCE	OPENNESS	OPTIMISM
ORDER	PATIENCE	PEACE	PERSEVERANCE	PLAYFULNESS
PLEASURE	POWER	PURITY	PURPOSE	RELAXATION
RELEASE	RENEWAL	RESOLUTION	RESPITE	RESPONSIBILITY
REST	SAFETY	SECURITY	SELF RELIANCE	SENSITIVITY
SIMPLICITY	SKILL	SPONTANEITY	STABILITY	STAMINA
STRENGTH	SURRENDER	SYMPATHY	TALENT	TENDERNESS
TRANQUILLITY	TRUST	TRUTH	UNDERSTANDING	VITALITY
WELL-BEING	WILLINGNESS	WISDOM	WONDER	ZEST

Multi-sensory activities

It's not just about looking and copying, it's about feeling too.

PAUL CÉZANNE

We have looked separately (or as separately as possible) at the different representational systems and ways of generating activities in the classroom which emphasise one sense more than the others. It is important when working in this way to ensure that over time – even during each lesson – we use a balance of activities, unless we happen to be working with an individual to correct an existing imbalance.

There is a lot of research which indicates that multi-sensory teaching is more effective and more memorable than anything else. I stand a much better chance of retaining something if I learn it through several systems at the same time rather than just one: redundancy means that if one of those systems fails me when I come to access that information, one of the others may work. If I only *see* something, I may or may not remember it. If I see it, hear it and feel it (in a psychomotor, tactile or visceral way), I am more likely to be able to access it when I need to.

'VAK' also relates to Howard Gardner's theory of Multiple Intelligences, according to which, intelligence is not just a question of **linguistic** or **logical/mathematical** aptitude, which forms the basis of most IQ tests and much classroom practice. We can be intelligent in many different ways and we all have different strengths and weaknesses. Gardner talks about six other intelligences which educators need to engage if they are to get their message across to everyone: **visual spatial** (relating to fashion, the arts, film), **musical**, **interpersonal** (communicating with others, eg through public relations, sociology), **intrapersonal** (psychology, theology), **naturalist** (anatomy, earth sciences, nutrition) and **bodily-kinaesthetic** (dance, sports, practical handicrafts, etc). Again this is about taking account of differences and not putting people into boxes. There may be other intelligences, and each intelligence can be sub-divided into many different specific skills.

There is a further rationale for multi-sensory teaching in whole-brain learning theory. Roger Sperry suggested in the late 60s that the two hemispheres of the brain are responsible for very different functions, the left being very much the logical, linear, analytical, linguistic and verbal hemisphere, and the right being the intuitive, imaginative, emotional, musical, poetic and artistic hemisphere. More recent research suggests that the division of labour between the two hemispheres is not as rigid as that proposed by Sperry and that there is anyway a great deal of interconnection between them. The implications, however, remain: that we need to stimulate the whole brain in our teaching, and not focus mainly (or solely) on left brain functions as much traditional teaching has done.

In terms of language teaching, we know that students learn most easily if they hear new language, say it out loud themselves, see it written down and write it themselves. These activities will vary in importance for different students. By incorporating more varied input relating to different senses and different intelligence types, we offer our students more effective learning opportunities.

The next group of activities engages all three major senses together or leads learners from one of the external senses to internal experience.

NLP music   Listen out together with your students for songs with a strong NLP theme. For example, *'Music of the Night'* from *Phantom of the Opera* by Andrew Lloyd Webber is full of multi-sensory and mixed-sensory language.

Favourites   Give students one or more of the questionnaires below to remind them to experience things through their different senses. Ask them to compare their answers. You can use different sorts of questions to practise different tenses. For example, you could give students the 'Friday questions' and ask them to turn them into 'Monday questions' by asking about the weekend using the past simple.

Favourites

Choose a place you really like. _____

What is the most beautiful sight in this place? _____

What sound do you like most there? _____

What's your main feeling about the place? _____

What's your favourite smell in this place? _____

What's the favourite taste associated with this place? _____

What is one other thing that makes this a favourite place? _____

Friday questions

What is the most interesting thing you've seen this week? _____

What is the strangest sound you've heard? _____

What is the most interesting thing you've touched or held in your hands? _____

What is the strongest feeling you've felt? _____

What is the nicest thing you've smelt? _____

What is the most delicious thing you've eaten or drunk? _____

Look and guess   Working in pairs, students use the questions below to guess different things about each other. Afterwards they compare their guesses.

Look and guess

Look at your partner and guess:

their favourite colour _____   their least favourite colour _____

their favourite type of music _____   their least favourite type of music _____

a physical activity they love _____   a physical activity they hate _____

their favourite smell _____   their least favourite smell _____

their favourite taste _____   their least favourite taste _____

Write down your guesses and check with your partner to see if you were right.

Taste and imagine   Bring in some sweets, biscuits or small pieces of dried fruit and give one to each student. Tell students that as they taste the item, to allow that taste to bring to mind an image of a person together with the sound of that person's voice and any feelings they have in connection with that person.

Afterwards students give a VAK description of their person to their partner, possibly following up with a written description.

With an advanced class, this activity might be linked to a reading activity using the extract from *In Search of Lost Time* by Marcel Proust (printed in *In Your Hands*), where he describes dunking a madeleine (a small cake) into his tea and the taste of it opening the door to a flood of memories. This might lead to group discussion of similar experiences that the students have had themselves in their lives.

This activity works particularly well with the senses of smell and taste as these seem to be linked directly to a particular area of the brain which stores memories. For smells, bring into the classroom a spice jar, perfume bottle, citrus fruit, or aromatherapy oil and pass it round the class or even light an incense stick or perfumed candle. We have also discovered scented board pens and a commercial pack of 'smells' – including 'tiger'! What images, sounds and feelings are generated?

It is of course possible to try the activity by stimulating the other senses. For sight or touch, hand round a piece of silk or velvet, a woollen sock, a ball, a beanbag or any one of a number of tactile objects. What memories are recalled? What sounds are associated? What internal feelings are generated?

For sound, play a piece of music that you think will be familiar to everyone in the class. This might even be the theme tune from a well-known TV programme or the soundtrack from a film. Or play a sound effect on cassette: birdsong, crickets chirping, heavy rainfall, cows mooing … whatever. What pictures come to mind? What feelings? What smells? What tastes?

Show a painting   There are some wonderful narrative paintings, especially of mythological themes. Ones we have used include Titian's *Bacchus and Ariadne* and Dalí's *Metamorphosis of Narcissus*. Use postcards from art galleries or pictures from art books, whatever you can get hold of. Use a colour photocopier to enlarge them or make colour transparencies (the latter is easier to see, but can be rather expensive). It is also exciting to get students to invent stories around more abstract paintings such as Kandinsky's *Cossacks*. What sounds, tactile sensations, feelings, smells and tastes do they associate with the painting?

VAKOG word association   Students work in small groups of three to five.

The first person begins the process by saying something visual, eg *'I can see a tree'*.

The second person responds to 'tree' by saying something associated with it, but in the auditory channel, eg *'I can hear a bird'*.

The third person responds with something kinaesthetic, eg *'I feel as if I'm flying through the air'*.

The fourth person (who may be the first person again) says something olfactory, eg *'I can smell the sea'*.

The next person says something gustatory, eg *'I can taste salt'*.

Then back to visual again … and so on until someone is unable to continue.

Purpose

To enhance enjoyment of the language.

Language focus

Vocabulary, spelling.

PROCEDURE

♦ Tell students that (according to Godfrey Smith in *Beyond the Tingle Quotient*) these are some of the most attractive words in the English language:

shimmer	*murmur*	*darling*
silken	*willow*	*golden*
caress	*tranquil*	*crystal*
mellifluous	*peace*	*autumn*

♦ Ask students to think first individually, and then to discuss in pairs:

• Which are your favourites? Put them in order. Why do you like them?
  Is it the look of the word on paper?
  Is it the sound of the word as you say it?
  Is it the feeling that you get about what the word represents?
  Is there another reason?

• Are there any words here that you don't like? Why not?

• Add three (or more) words you really like. And a few words you don't like. Think about why.

♦ Ask students – individually – to choose one word they like most of all and to write it down. They then mime it to their partner who must guess what it is. Invite students in turn to say their words out loud (and check by asking: *Can anyone remember Paulo's word?* etc).

♦ Students work with a partner and make a sentence containing both their words – again reading/acting out their sentence for the rest of the class to enjoy.

> *Summer afternoon – summer afternoon; to me those have always been the two most beautiful words in the English language.*
>
> HENRY JAMES

> *I like the shape the word 'elbow' makes on the page.*
>
> DENNIS POTTER, TELEVISION PLAYWRIGHT.

Taking account of students'
INDIVIDUALITY and DIFFERENCES

So you're much more aware of how different people are, but you've still got to teach them all in one class. You've got students at different language levels, with differing degrees of motivation, with different interests, working at different speeds. How can you cater for their individual needs? Try some or all of the following.

- Teach or check a specific vocabulary area with a picture that everyone can see (eg on the OHP or in the textbook), then ask students to imagine their own picture in their heads. With a partner, or as a mingle, they discuss the differences between their internal pictures.

- Tell students what you're doing and why. Make them aware of the things you are doing which will help them learn. Give them the skills to use for themselves. Give them a lesson plan and timetable for the week, the term, the course. Better still, involve them, as a class activity, in planning the work.

- Have time out. Have an occasional two-minute break in a lesson when people can do anything they like (as long as they don't make too much noise).

- Offer a choice, eg ask students to learn 10 out of a possible 30 items of vocabulary, or answer any 10 out of 12 questions.

- Students take more responsibility for their learning by marking their homework before they hand it in. You will have less to mark and will see which students might need personal attention when their mark differs wildly from yours.

- Ask students for their opinions, reactions and preferences. Ask them what they really think and feel, rather than asking for the fixed textbook responses.

- Use stories from students' own experience rather than stories from the textbook.

- Use lots of the activities suggested in 'Pandora's Box' on page 30.

- Do relaxation exercises and guided fantasies. From the same input from you, each person does something very different in the privacy of their own heads.

- Learn about metaprograms and VAK so that you are aware of many of the possibilities. Take account of them, particularly by using appropriate language.

- Gradually build up a series of self-access workcards on different subjects (vocabulary areas, pronunciation, punctuation, grammar practice, writing a poem, etc). Occasionally have a lesson where students choose what they work on.

- Occasionally offer tasks at three levels (easy, medium and advanced) related to the same input. Allow students to choose which one(s) they do.

- Give students the responsibility of finding and/or checking their own answers.

- Ask student to set tasks and tests, and make up activities for one another.

- When you set up a task, or ask a question of the group, give a moment's private thinking time before students start the task or you accept an answer.

- Ask students to make up their own tasks and exercises based on material in the textbook. Use the tasks with other classes.

- Do exercises which help students understand why they behave as they do, and what motivates them – like 'significant words' on the next page.

SIGNIFICANT WORDS

Purpose

To help students understand what motivates them.

Language focus

Any; cause and effect.

PROCEDURE

- Ask students individually to make a note of six moments when they have heard something, read something or someone has said something to them which has had a significant effect on them. Ask for six moments, but stop when most people have got two or three. Ask them to write down the exact words which had an effect.

- Students work in small groups. In turn, they show their words, the others guess the circumstances and the effect they had. The student accepts right guesses and, after the others have made a few suggestions, corrects any wrong impressions. All members of the group then discuss what they think the student is most motivated by, eg fear of failure, needing to be liked, wanting to succeed, wanting to impress others, wanting to prove someone wrong, etc. Set a time limit of five minutes per person, and keep time strictly.

- Students take different situations and decide what words they might say to each of the others which would be the most likely to make them act. Either take one situation at random and each person writes down the words they would say to each of the others, or choose one student and one situation: everyone writes down the words they would say to that student. The student also writes down the words they think might have the most effect. Situations might include:

> *What words would you say to ...*
> *get them to get out of bed in the morning?*
> *get them to go out when they wanted to stay in and study?*
> *get them to take their turn at paying for a shared meal?*
> *get them to help you tidy your room?*
> *get them to go with you to a film they've already seen?*
> *help them to have the courage to talk to someone they really fancy?*
> *help them confess to damaging a shirt they've borrowed from a friend?*

- At the end of the activity, each student individually writes down three things they have learnt about what motivates them to do things, and for each motivator, they write down three specific ways in which that might help them. For example, one student wrote:

> *I react very well to pressure, but I don't start doing anything until the very last minute. This is sometimes a problem if something unexpected happens. I need to remind myself to leave time for the unexpected. I would also enjoy my weekends more if I did my homework on a Friday and then had the whole weekend free to enjoy myself. I know I won't do that. However, I think I will spend 15 minutes on a Friday evening looking through my homework, so that I know exactly how much work I've got to do and I can plan better.*

Purpose

To help students understand what motivates them.

Language focus

Agreeing/disagreeing.

PROCEDURE

- Tell students you are going to give them a series of opposing statements about their own behaviour. You will point to one side of the room when you say one sentence and the other side of the room when you say the opposite sentence. Students must go to the side of the room whose sentence better reflects the truth about their behaviour.

- Read out the pairs of sentences on the metaprograms worksheet. Students should first commit themselves to one side or the other and discuss (in English) with the people they find themselves with how this sentence affects their behaviour and what it means in practice. Ask them then to stand somewhere between the two statements to show how strongly they agree with the statement on a sliding scale. Then read out the next statement.

- When students have responded to all eight statements, give them the worksheet and ask them to fill it in for themselves.

- Students then mingle to try to find other people with exactly the same profile as themselves (it is unlikely that many people will find someone with exactly the same profile). They must speak to one another in English without showing anyone else their completed worksheet.

- After about five minutes, have a class discussion about what this means for them as a group of learners.

Comment

Explain to students what metaprograms are. Once our brain finds a way of behaving that works, it tends to repeat it, so that it becomes a habit, or a program. The non-conscious filters our brains habitually use to select relevant information from our sensory experience are called 'metaprograms' in NLP. People tend to believe that the way they think is the way everyone thinks – or the way all intelligent people should think. In many cases, people are prepared to compromise and work together relatively well, however it can be frustrating when other people in a group work in very different ways from us, and occasionally the situation can become very uncomfortable (and not conducive to learning) if two people with strongly opposing methods of working have to work together.

Once people are aware that others are not just being 'difficult', but that their brains actually work in a different way, they are usually willing to be more accommodating – or at least agree to work separately with fewer hard feelings. Remember that when you say someone is 'difficult', you usually mean that they don't want to do things your way.

Know thyself!

PLATO

METAPROGRAMS

Grade yourself according to how strongly you agree with the statements on each side of the scale.

1 I like to think before I act   O   O   O   O   O   O   I don't like wasting time. I like to get on with the job.

2 I like people to praise me.   O   O   O   O   O   O   I know when I've done well. I don't need others to tell me.

3 I like someone to tell me exactly how to do things.   O   O   O   O   O   O   I like experimenting and doing things my way.

4 I work best when I know what the reward is.   O   O   O   O   O   O   I only start working when I'm scared of what will happen if I don't.

5 I like new things all the time.   O   O   O   O   O   O   I like to do things I know.

6 I concentrate most on my own needs.   O   O   O   O   O   O   I can only work well when everyone around me is happy.

7 I work better on my own.   O   O   O   O   O   O   I work better as part of a team.

8 I can't work until I've worked through the details of how to do something.   O   O   O   O   O   O   I need to have an overview before I look at details.

There are no difficult students –
just students who don't want to do it your way.

Yes, but ...

These activities won't work with:

- teenagers
- beginners
- business people
- large classes
- one-to-one
- my students!

Yes, and ...

Choose the answers which are most helpful to you.

1 You're right. Give this book to someone else with the right sort of students.

2 Justify yourself. Write down ten reasons why these activities wouldn't work with your students. When you've finished, read through your list. Ask your non-conscious mind to suggest ways to make them work. Forget about it. Go and do something else.

3 Yes they will … especially if you want them to. Imagine you are a wise and experienced teacher (an easy thing to do). Suggest ways of adapting the activities to work with these students. (Think of specific suggestions for each of your reasons in number 2.)

4 Share this book with a colleague. Plan together how to use specific activities with specific classes. Afterwards, compare how things went and how you could improve next time.

5 Go through *Handing Over* grading the activities:

(✓) I could do it now (with a particular class).

(✗) I could never do this in a million years.

(?) Maybe I could do this if … (suggest ways of changing the activity)

(☝) I love this activity. Somehow I'll find a way to make it work for my students.

6 Choose a 'never-in-a-million-years' activity. We challenge you to make it work with your most difficult group of students. Please write and tell us how it went!

7 We've tried out all these activities with a wide range of students. We often adapt them slightly (or significantly) for different students. Other people have tried them too. The activities do work.

8 You might find some of the activities a bit demanding initially, but you have the skills to make them work with your students.

9 Write your own answers to the question here.

_____

_____

_____

_____

_____

You might be interested to look back at these answers and find which ones are motivating for you and which aren't. Use the information to motivate yourself to do other things you want to achieve. (Does this page give you any ideas about an approach you could take to motivate students?)

Learning by heart

Learning by heart went out of fashion. It implied that students could get away with not understanding the meaning – and anyway, it was 'difficult'. Today, though, everyone's talking about 'chunking' – learning contextualised chunks of language rather than (or as well as) individual words or grammatical structures. As long as the chunks learnt are relevant to the student in some way, learning by heart can be an important asset – and it's so easy if you take a multi-sensory approach. It is not necessary for students to have 'learnt' all the structures in the text, as long as they understand the meaning.

- It builds confidence.
- The techniques will stand students in good stead for learning anything all their lives (lists of facts, lines for acting in a play, etc).
- The text provides language models which can later be analysed or incorporated into a more structured model.
- It helps them to 'get their tongue round' the language and improves pronunciation.

Use the story on the next page to learn the technique, then prepare a relevant text of your own (maybe from your coursebook) and ask students to organise themselves to learn it. In the first instance, use the complete sequence of activities. However, this is probably overkill. Once students know the activities, you (they) will be able to use fewer of them and still be confident of learning the text. You will also find many of the individual activities usable within the scope of other lessons.

MEMORISE A TEXT

Preparation of the text

Choose a short text or divide a longer text into chunks. Write it out in short lines, one sentence or phrase at a time, in large letters. Make one copy per student. Prepare a flip chart pad (or the board) with the sample illustrations on the grid (see page 70). Prepare a second, empty copy of the grid.

PROCEDURE

- The activity assumes a group of between 12 and 60 learners at low to middle intermediate level or above, any age group above 12.
- It is not necessary for students to try to learn the text by heart. It will happen easily if they follow this procedure.

1 Dramatic introduction

With the grid visible, read the text aloud, line by line, acting it out dramatically with extravagant gestures and intonation. Be prepared to look a bit silly. (You may even like to be 'suggestopedic' and play some background music.)

2 Listen and repeat – with attitude

Read the text to the students, one line at a time. (They do not yet have the text.) They repeat exactly what you say. Follow this sequence, be very precise, and exaggerate what you are doing:

- Look at your copy of the text and silently read the first line.
- Clasp your text to your chest.
- Silently repeat the line to yourself, looking up towards the ceiling and moving your lips to show the students what is going on.
- Say the line really dramatically while making eye contact with the students.
- Point to the students and cover your mouth to indicate that now they should silently repeat the line in their heads while looking up to the ceiling. Ask them to 'see' the line and 'hear' themselves saying it with exactly the same intonation as the model.
- At your signal, the students chorus the line together with the same dramatic intonation.
- Repeat with the next line – and subsequent lines – in the same way.

If students are not copying the intonation and speed of the model exactly (or even if they are), just to keep motivation high, play about with it. Say a couple of words very quickly for them to repeat. Then a sentence in a very high voice. Then different words very slowly – like a robot – like a police siren – all on one note, etc. If they don't copy exactly, do it again. Exaggerate. Keep it fun. When you've said it in a 'silly' way, put it back together and give a good model for them to repeat before moving on.

3 Check the picture grid

See how much of the text students can remember so far. With your hand over your mouth to indicate that they shouldn't speak yet, point at each picture and give people the chance to remember the words. At your signal, everyone says the words they remember. Do not give the correct version. Do not judge in any way. Just give everyone the chance to try to remember as much as they can, link the words with the pictures, and hear what the other students are saying.

4 Individual speaking

Give students their own copy of the text. Students follow the sequence you demonstrated before: they read a line, clasp the text to their chest, hear themselves saying the line silently in their heads while looking up, and then say the words aloud. Once they have learnt this sequence, they roam around the room (or stand up in their places, turning in different directions) saying the text aloud in a variety of different ways. Tell them to be as silly as possible (or give instructions, such as 'whisper', 'loudly', 'v..e..r..y s..l..o..w..l..y', 'in a deep sexy voice', etc). Everyone is speaking at once, but at their own pace. To make sure students don't try to chorus the lines together, start them off by pointing quickly at different people to get them going at different times.

Students have the opportunity to get their tongues around the words in the 'privacy' afforded by everyone speaking at once. Since they are being instructed to speak in a silly way, they will succeed in the task if they make 'silly' mistakes – and they will also succeed if they say it right.

5 Individuals speaking to one another

Repeat the previous activity (4), but this time they interact with one another. Saying lines of the text, they make eye contact with someone else and pretend to be having a conversation by using an interactive intonation pattern.

6 Listen and repeat with your partner

The class divides into two equal groups which line up on opposite sides of the room. They make eye contact with the person opposite them who becomes their partner. They follow the sequence you established when you asked them to copy you (Acitivity 2). They take turns with each line to be leader and follower. The follower does not look at the text. The leader reads one line silently, clasps the text to their chest, makes eye contact with their partner, and speaks the line. The partner says the line silently to themselves and then repeats aloud as exactly as possible. 'Silly' intonation is encouraged.

Everyone is talking at the same time, which demands total concentration between the partners, but amazingly they are able to hear one another. The key thing is that people standing next to one another are at different points in the sequence, so you should start pairs off at different times by pointing very quickly at different people on different sides of the room.

7 Repeat step 3

… with everyone sitting back in their places. Start by pointing at the pictures in the grid in the correct order and then start jumping around. By now, most people will have memorised most of the text. Remember to leave thinking time before indicating that everyone speak together.

8 Repeat step 7

… using – but only pointing at – the empty grid. It's amazing how much people can remember just by looking at the empty squares – and also how useful it is to look at the empty squares.

9 Written test

Students write the text word for word under 'test' conditions. This is simply to give them the satisfaction of realising how much they have learnt without any effort. They check their own text against the original and correct any mistakes.

10 Revision

Leave the pictures and the grid up on the wall for the next week and occasionally ask individuals or the class to say the phrase represented by one picture and/or the whole text.

Comment

If you use this technique for a different text, make sure that the grid has a different and appropriate layout.

The Monk and the Thief

The Monk and the Thief

1   *A thief was once watching a very holy monk through a hole in the wall.*

2   *As he watched, the monk walked straight through a solid brick wall into the next room.*

3   *'Now that would be a very useful skill,' thought the thief to himself.*

4   *He went to the monk and said, 'Master, would you please teach me to walk through walls?'*

5   *'Certainly,' said the monk. 'If you become my pupil and do everything I tell you, you will learn to walk through walls.'*

6   *The thief did everything the monk asked for a year and then he asked, 'Master, when will you teach me to walk through walls?'*

7   *'If you continue to do everything I tell you, you will learn to walk through walls,' said the monk.*

8   *The thief did everything the monk asked for five years and then he asked, 'Master, when will you teach me to walk through walls?'*

9   *'If you continue to do everything I tell you, you will learn to walk through walls,' said the monk.*

10 *The thief did everything the monk asked for ten years and then he asked, 'Master, when will you teach me to walk through walls?'*

11 *'If you continue to do everything I tell you, you will learn to walk through walls,' said the monk.*

12 *A few years later, the thief wanted something from the next room, so he walked through the wall to fetch it.*

13 *He didn't even notice.*

Metaphor

By metaphor, we mean any word or phrase which links one idea with another; we are not limiting it to its strict literary meaning. Language is intrinsically metaphorical, and the way we speak reflects the way we experience, think and talk about the world.

Conversely, metaphors shape the way that we think about the world and therefore the way that we behave in relation to it. Positive metaphors can greatly enhance our experience. Negative metaphors can undermine our potential. For example, my teaching is likely to be very different if I think of it as a 'journey of discovery' rather than as a 'daily battle'. Exploring new metaphors enables us to understand and appreciate things in new ways, and if we change our metaphors, we can change the way we think and behave. Once we make a link between two things by means of a fruitful metaphor, it is hard to go back entirely to our old way of thinking.

Stories, of course, are usually extended metaphors – and we have dedicated a separate section to them (see page 83).

METAPHORICAL LANGUAGE

Purpose
To help students become aware of the metaphorical use of everyday language.

Language focus
Idioms.

PROCEDURE

- Give students the photocopiable page (page 73) to complete in pairs or small groups. They can use dictionaries to look up expressions they don't know.

- Ask students to compare the idioms with similar (or different) concepts in their own language.

- You (or students) may be able to think of other extended metaphors. 'Up' and 'down', for example, are very commonly used to represent happiness, health and life versus sickness and death (rise from the dead, fall ill, in tiptop shape, to drop dead, to come down with flu, his health is declining), etc.

ANSWERS TO WORKSHEET ON PAGE 73

1 up = happiness 2 down = misery 3 time = money 4 understanding = light 5 love = war
6 ideas = food 7 theory = building 8 life = gambling

METAPHORICAL LANGUAGE

Consider the following groups of idioms. Which concept is being described? What is the concept being compared to?

1   I'm feeling up, in high spirits, on top of the world.
    That's really boosted my morale; I've reached the height of ecstasy; I'm on cloud nine.
    Concept _____ *UP* _____ = _____ *HAPPINESS* _____

2   She's feeling down, depressed, low. She's sinking (falling) into a depression. In fact she's hit rock bottom.
    Concept _____ = _____

3   Could you spare me a moment? I know you think it's a waste of time, but it will be time well spent.
    You've earned some time off and this is a real time saver. Last month's mistake cost us three weeks.
    Concept _____ = _____

4   It came to me in a flash. I saw the light and my eyes were opened. It was blindingly obvious.
    Now let's shed some light on the subject and clear up this misunderstanding.
    Concept _____ = _____

5   She had many conquests and was besieged by suitors. She was fending off admirers. He pursued her relentlessly.
    She fled from his advances. He made an ally of her mother and began to feel he was gaining ground.
    Eventually she was overpowered by love and he won her hand in marriage.
    Concept _____ = _____

6   I'm a voracious reader, and I can devour a book at one sitting. This book has given me food for thought.
    It's something I can really get my teeth into. It's going to take me a while to digest it all, but it's really meaty.
    I need to chew it over a bit, but at least I'm not being spoon fed with half-baked ideas that I can't swallow.
    Concept _____ = _____

7   You've got a good framework, but now you need to construct a strong argument to support your theory. You haven't got
    enough solid facts. Your proof is very shaky and it will fall apart under criticism. I'm afraid it's all going to collapse.
    Concept _____ = _____

8   The odds are stacked against me, and my opponent is holding all the cards. I'll take my chances and up the ante.
    I think he's bluffing, so I'll play it close to my chest, knowing that I've got an ace up my sleeve.
    When the chips are down, it's just the luck of the draw, after all. I'm not a loser. It's a toss up as to whether I win or lose.
    Concept _____ = _____

FIND THE LINK

Purpose
To help students think about the similarities and connections between one thing and another.

Language focus
Comparisons.

Preparation
Prepare a set of about 20 cards for every six students in the class with words or pictures on them. Make your own or photocopy pages 75-78.

PROCEDURE

- Give each group of six students a set of cards divided in two and placed in two piles face down.

- Write on the board the prompts:

    Both of them are/have/can ...

    Neither of them is/has/can ...

- Students take it in turns to turn over one card from each pile. Everyone in the group has two minutes to write down as many comparisons as possible between the two things. Comparisons can be positive or negative.

- Students read out and compare their sentences, starting with the student who turned over the cards. Students score two points for every comparison which no-one else has made, one point for a comparison which only one other person has made. The cards are put to the bottom of the piles and the next student turns over two cards.

- Give five minutes' notice that the activity is going to end. The winner is the student with the most points.

Variation

- At lower levels use only pictures.

- In a more advanced version of the game, there is one pile of picture cards of concrete objects (see pages 76-77), and a second pile of cards of abstract words (see pages 75 and 78), both face down. In this version, the 'game' element frequently gets lost as a deeper discussion takes over.

    Students work in groups of three: **A**, **B** and **C**. **A** picks up an abstract word card and reads it out. **B** picks up a concrete object card and compares it to the abstract object, saying *'x is like a ...'*. **C** says *'because ...'*, and gives a reason. Next time round, **B** starts, then **C**, etc.

life	death	marriage	career
learning	health	education	teaching
ownership	relationships	communication	language
property	responsibility	sex	partnership
rights	leisure	work	consideration

holiday	honour	guilt	faithfulness
belief	spirituality	self	loss
maturity	fear	security	bravery
self esteem	being a teenager	growing up	English
testing	respect	courtesy	comfort

CREATIVE METAPHORS

Purpose

To use metaphorical comparisons to help problem-solving; creative thinking.

Language focus

Adjectives.

PROCEDURE

- The class identifies an interesting but unusual idea. For example, how would it be if people preferred weeds to cultivated flowers? Or what would happen if people could choose which side of the road they drive on? Or how would society be different if poverty was valued over wealth?

- Students work in small groups and choose a concrete noun totally at random (perhaps by taking one of the picture cards on pages 76-77). They brainstorm ways of describing the object they have chosen in as many different ways as possible in a given amount of time (about five minutes). For the object 'ball', you might think of: *catch it, throw it, hit it, it's round, it might bounce, you play games with it, it rolls, kick it, it can float, you write numbers on it and have it in a lottery, you juggle with it, you keep it in the air, you drop it, players need to be physically dexterous,* etc.

- Students then link the descriptions of the object to the challenging situation to help them see its possibilities. For example, if people could choose which side of the road to drive on, and the object is a ball:

  - *driving might become more like a game*
  - *you might need to have rubber cars which could bounce off each other*
  - *you might need to have tracks that cars roll along*
  - *people might often get out of their cars and hit or kick each other*
  - *a lot more people might decide to catch a train or a bus*
  - *more people might take up ballooning so they could float above the traffic*

- The aim is to get people thinking in new, creative ways, making links between things they had not previously connected, generating language, and coming up with innovative ideas. For example, it might well be helpful to the traffic situation if more people caught buses and trains, and there might be fewer accidents if people had to drive their cars along predetermined tracks – which could be on any side of the road because there would be no danger of people doing something unpredictable and hitting one another.

Variation

- When students understand how the activity works, they can apply a similar technique to solving problems. Groups can work on the same problem or different problems. Either the whole class chooses one object or each group can have a different object.

Purpose

To help students gain useful insights into what helps them learn.

Language focus

Any.

PROCEDURE

- Write up on the board 'animal, vegetable or mineral', and check that students know that everything can be divided into these three categories. Give two or three examples of things and ask students to categorise them. Ask for two or three further examples of each.

- Ask students to think about you as a teacher. Working in small groups of four or five, they have got five minutes to decide on three metaphors which represent you as a teacher: one animal, one vegetable, one mineral.

- Groups tell you their metaphors and you write them on the board. Thank them and tell them that you'll certainly think about their metaphors and gain insights from them.

- Tell students that they're going to think of three metaphors for themselves. Advise them to accept the first thing that comes into their minds as it has probably come from their non-conscious mind. Then write on the board, 'Three metaphors for me as a learner', and say clearly, 'Write down three metaphors for yourself as a learner. One animal, one vegetable and one mineral.'

- Students share their metaphors in pairs or small groups. (You can add a 'K' element and some fun by asking students to mime one of their metaphors for the others to guess.)

- Students discuss the attributes of the different metaphors. What do they show about the different ways we learn? What are the positive things about each metaphor? What does it tell us about ourselves as learners? Is there anything about the metaphor (ours, or someone else's) which suggests ways in which we could learn more effectively?

Comment

You might like to share Jane's experience with students to get them started. When Jane first thought about herself as a learner, she was dismayed when the image that popped into her mind was … an octopus! She had hoped for something a little more elegant, a swan perhaps, or a fox. But no, she got an octopus. It was only when she began to explore it that she realised what a good metaphor it is for learning: all those legs waving about in lots of different directions, and those big, big eyes could prove very useful indeed!

- Students draw a representation of their different metaphors, along with notes about the implications for themselves as learners.

Follow up

- Refer back to the metaphors after a few weeks. Ask students whether the metaphor has proved useful and whether they've discovered further links. (They can discuss this in small groups and report back to the class.)

Comment

Keep your responses light-hearted to the metaphors about you as a teacher, eg writing down the ones you like in big letters, or pulling funny faces for things you don't like so much. Make sure that you write down everything, even if you think it's unflattering. You will gain much more sympathy and support from the class as a whole if you are able to absorb criticism (whether warranted or not) from a few. The first part of the activity gets students thinking about metaphors and teaching, before they add the more difficult dimension of applying it to themselves.

In privacy, later, think about the metaphors students have offered you and learn from them — particularly the ones you don't like so much. Even if they were said 'as a joke', or because particular students don't get on well with you, there is almost certainly a grain of truth in what they say. If you don't get on well with particular students, you probably can't change their behaviour without first changing the way you behave towards them.

IF I WERE

Purpose

Awareness of self; awareness of metaphor.

Language focus

Second conditional; lexical sets.

PROCEDURE

● Write up on the board the key sentence:

If you were a/n ..., what kind of ... would you be?

Also write up five or six categories of vocabulary at random, eg *vegetable, transport, plant, water, animal, bird, house, room, furniture.*

● Brainstorm lots of examples of words in the different categories. If possible, use a large sheet of flip-chart paper and a different colour pen for each category.

● Students work in small groups of four or five. Each group has a bilingual dictionary which they can use to check words that nobody in the group knows.

● Students take turns to choose a category, and ask the others the question, eg *'If you were an animal, what kind of animal would you be?'*

Each person thinks about the answer and then replies: *'I would be a horse'*, etc .

Groups discuss the answers, possibly offering alternative (preferably positive!) suggestions about how they see the person.

Variation

● In smaller classes, write the names of the categories on cards, one set per group. Instead of choosing, students turn over cards to determine the category.

● Prepare the brainstormed vocabulary items on small cards. Each group has a set of cards and organises the words into the relevant categories. This introduces quite a number of new vocabulary items before going into the activity.

How do I grade students using NLP?

There are almost certainly external factors determining the form in which you have to grade students, eg an evaluation system determined by the school, the state or the examination board. We strongly recommend you comply with this.

At the same time, however, there are ways of making grading and evaluation a more relevant learning activity for students.

• Involve them in the grading system. Explain what the imposed/external system is and what they have to do in order to achieve a pass mark or a high grade.

• Ask them to grade their own work. Every time they hand in a piece of work, ask them to write on it the grade they think they should receive. Strangely, most students are pretty honest and pretty accurate. You only need spend time discussing grades with students whose own estimate differs wildly from yours. We have often found that both we and the students have had to revise our grades in these situations – often students have a better idea of what they know than we do. On the other hand, we are able to explain to them how they can present their work so that other people can understand how much they know.

• Grading only tells students how well they have done up to now. When students do something well in particular tasks, ask them to explore how they managed to do it so well, and to share their strategies with other people to help their future learning. Not every strategy will work for everyone, but it's likely that someone will benefit every time.

• Provide (or develop with students) a grading system which is more precise than a number or letter of the alphabet. What does B+ actually mean? Try grading written work under the following headings, giving 20% for each:

Content & ideas, Grammar, Vocabulary, Punctuation & spelling, Presentation

• Explain (or elicit) a basic introduction to the components of language that you, the teacher, are taking into consideration. Ask students to grade themselves on each component and therefore identify areas they need to work on. Each individual profile will be different. (The discussion involved in this activity can raise a lot of issues about language learning and the respective roles of teachers and students.) Grading can be done regularly to indicate perceived progress.

The profile sheet will differ according to the age and language level of the students, but the following basic areas – with possible subdivisions in brackets – might give you some ideas to get you started:

Vocabulary (receptive, productive)

Grammar (structures, functions)

Reading (reading what? – simplified readers, newspapers, technical information?)

Listening (to what? the radio, pop songs, the teacher, native speakers, American movies?)

Writing (see grading list above)

Speaking (accuracy, fluency, pronunciation – stress, intonation, sounds)

Stories

Stories don't have a middle and an end.
They usually have a beginning that never stops beginning.

STEPHEN SPIELBERG

As language teachers we have always used stories: with children, with teenagers, with adults, with everyone. Why? Because they're such wonderful vehicles for language in a meaningful context. They're highly motivating, they engage the emotions and they seem to satisfy some deep psychological need for narrative. Whenever we announce that it's story time, our students always smile, sit back and relax … while being particularly attentive. We all love a good story.

Anchoring

It is a nice idea to 'anchor' the storytelling itself in some way. Jane has a storytelling shawl (given to her by a Russian lady called Lily). Every time she puts on the shawl, the group know they are in for a story and settle accordingly. (The group also know that if the shawl is passed to one of them, it's going to be their turn to tell a story!)

There are lots of ways you can anchor in order to get students into 'listening-to-a-story' mood. You could have a special storytelling chair that you only sit in when you tell a story. Or a special storytelling corner – as they often do in primary schools. Or you might light a candle or a joss stick; or have an auditory anchor such as a special piece of music that you play or chimes that you ring. And before you start the story, you might like to use the words from a famous radio programme for children: *'Are you sitting comfortably? Then I'll begin.'*

Stories as vehicles

Stories are vehicles for all kinds of different things.

- They are obviously **vehicles for language**: we can use them to present or practise grammatical structures, functions or vocabulary.

- They are also **vehicles for information and ideas** which can often be presented in an interesting and memorable way through some kind of story.

- They are **vehicles for messages**: often a story conveys a message metaphorically in a much more palatable and powerful way than a direct communication. These messages include moral messages and we need to be careful that the morals are ones we are happy for our students (or our children) to have.

- And they are **vehicles for values or beliefs**: stories often contain an underlying view of the world which is so integral to the story that we almost don't notice it. For example, many traditional children's stories involve a young woman who finds herself in deep trouble which she is unable to sort out herself, so she has to be rescued by a handsome prince. Are these the values and beliefs that we want our little girls to receive? Or our little boys?

We're not saying don't use traditional stories, but be aware of values which they may be promoting non-consciously. One strategy is to encourage listeners to search for alternative endings by asking questions like: *'Suppose the prince overslept that day, what might have happened instead?'* Or students can imagine characters taking different roles. Can they rewrite the story of *Little Red Riding Hood* so that the woodcutter is rescued by grandma, or even by the wolf? Or rewriting the story of the *Three Little Pigs* as a newspaper article: *'I was framed'* says A. Wolf. This type of approach enhances comprehension of the original, as well as being creative and thought-provoking.

♦ Like guided fantasies, stories are also **vehicles for multi-sensory imaginary experience**.

♦ Stories are **vehicles for embedded suggestions**. Use them to boost learners' confidence and their belief in themselves as learners and as people.

What is an embedded suggestion? Any direct suggestion that one character makes to another within a story can serve as an embedded suggestion to the non-conscious mind of your listeners or readers. For example

• The wise old man smiled and said, *'My dears, **it's in your hands**'.*

• The traveller thanked the villagers, *'Thank you for everything **you're teaching me.**'*

• *'I'm amazed at **how quickly you learn things**,'* the wizard said to her apprentice.

When a storyteller uses the words 'you', 'your', and so on, within a story, there are two receivers of the message. One is the character in the story, and the other is the storyteller's audience.

So how can you turn a simple direct suggestion from one character to another into an embedded suggestion for your audience? You need to mark it out in some way. In speech, this means changing your voice to give the words special emphasis. In writing, it means using graphic devices (italics, bold, a different typeface, inverted commas, etc) to mark out what you want to be noticed.

♦ Remember too that stories are actually **vehicles for sheer enjoyment**. If you are dissecting a story to work on vocabulary or grammar, remember to put it back together again at the end by reading the story aloud. And sometimes, tell students a story just for fun. No exploitation of language, no searching for messages – sheer pleasure!

Getting into a story

There are lots of ways to involve students in stories. The following ideas can be used before telling a story to awaken students' interest, or encourage them to write stories of their own. Either way, they will usually be interested to hear your version.

Here is a list of possible ways into a story (which we're sure you can add to). The way you choose will depend very much on your story. Where we mention particular stories, we have chosen ones that are likely to be fairly well known universally, such as myths, legends and fairy tales, though the techniques work with any sorts of story and also with songs, poems and other texts from your coursebook.

Sensory approaches

♦ (V) **Show a picture** or a series of pictures. To add interest, cover a crucial part of the picture (eg on an OHP) and ask students to speculate about the missing part. With a series of pictures, eg a cartoon strip, make sure you don't show the last one too soon. As soon as they know the end, interest will flag. Ask what sounds, tactile sensations, feelings, smells and tastes they associate with the picture.

- (V) **Show pictures of the main character** or characters. These might be types rather than specific characters, for example a king, a princess, a wizard, a witch, a blacksmith, a sailor, a fox, etc. Students speculate on different storylines before they hear or read the story.

- (VK) **Mime** – or better still get students to mime – either the whole story, or the general idea, or a particular scene from the story, for the class to guess what is happening. With or without sound effects.

- (A) **Play appropriate music** from the period if you have it, Elizabethan music for a story from Shakespeare, for example, or a song or theme music from a relevant film or musical, such as *Titanic,* or *West Side Story.* Soundtracks from famous television programmes may be useful too: well-known hospital drama music for a hospital story like the one on page 36, for example. The music can be used to stimulate interest in the story – what images, tactile sensations, feelings, smells and tastes do they imagine? And/or it can be played as background music to the telling of the story and subsequent activities.

- (A) **Use sound effects**. You can use cassettes, but it is often more fun if you (or the students) produce your own sound effects. Try baa-ing like a sheep for *The Boy Who Cried Wolf*, quacking like *The Ugly Duckling*, or asking students to find the most realistic way of representing the sound of the sea, or weather effects, etc.

- (V/K+O/G) **Show students real objects.** Bring in feathers for the story of *Icarus*, for example, or a basket of goodies for *Little Red Riding Hood*, or a tub of ice for a trek to the North Pole. Have students touch and feel things rather than just look at them. Or ask them to predict what the story might be about from a smell (flowers, antiseptic, pine) or taste (fruit juice, chocolate, cheese, etc).

- (V and/or A, O or G) **Focus on the geographical location.** Use a combination of maps, national music and typical smells or tastes to evoke the provenance of a story. For the story of Asclepius (on page 88), for example, you might use a map of Greece to show the location of Athens and Piraeus, plus postcards or pictures from travel magazines (or our photos). Play some Greek music, bring in some oregano for them to smell, and olives for them to taste.

All these things are a useful external sensory prelude to them working on their internal sensory representations as they listen to the story.

Verbal approaches

There are also of course many other ways into a story involving words (either spoken or written). We include them for the sake of completeness, and partly as a reminder that the ideas in this book are offered as complementary to whatever other activities and approaches you are using with your students.

Give students one or more of the following: the title, words taken from the story, the first line(s), an isolated sentence within the story, questions on the story, speculative questions, the moral(s), the theme (eg revenge), the historical or socio-political context. Ask them to imagine or guess things such as the storyline, the title, the characters, words that will or won't occur, the beginning, the ending …

Different interpretations

Bear in mind that no story ever has just one message or moral. Although that may or may not be the intention of the writer or teller, the reader or listener always brings their own map of the world into the interpretation. And the more deeply metaphorical the story, the more numerous will be the interpretations of it.

While it is perfectly valid to ask for the 'teacher's interpretation' of the story (which is presumably also the examiners' interpretation), remember to ask for (and accept) alternative meanings. Try it now for yourself with the Asclepius story (on page 88).

What do you think is the main message?

Can you find at least three other possible messages? (These might not be as obvious as your first message, so open your mind to other possibilities.)

─────────────── POSSIBLE MESSAGES ───────────────

- One's view of places (and probably people, and even life in general) is coloured much more by one's own perception and expectations, than by anything intrinsic about the place itself. (Probably this is most people's main message.)
- Asclepius was a wise man who realised that his view would not necessarily be that of the travellers, so he did not attempt to impose his view on them.
- Asclepius didn't answer because he didn't know what Athens was like.
- Asclepius didn't want to be helpful.
- Maybe very different things had happened to the two travellers in Piraeus to make them have such different views of the city. One might have been attacked and robbed, while the other might have won the lottery – neither event was necessarily anything to do with the city.
- Maybe the two travellers lived in two very different parts of Piraeus.
- All three of the characters were very lucky that neither of the other two was a murderous thug. Maybe life was safer at the time of the story.
- Find out about a place before you set off.
- Only men go walking in the Greek countryside.
- If you want an answer to a question, don't ask Asclepius.

ATHENS

86

MULTI-SENSORY STORY TELLING

Purpose

To encourage students to become aware of the different representational systems.

Language focus

Comprehension; adjectives; adverbs.

PROCEDURE

- Students read a story which contains few descriptive passages (such as the Asclepius story on the next page).

- Students work in small groups to write in as much description as possible. This can take the form of simply adding adjectives and adverbs, or students can be more creative and add whole descriptive passages.

- Each group reads their version of the story to the others.

Variations

- Different groups of students add descriptions from a different sense (VAKOG).

- Students must add descriptions relating to each sense – possibly in a given order.

- The different variations can be given to different groups in a multi-level class, ie lower level groups add any description they like, high level groups add descriptions relating to each sense in a prescribed order, etc.

- Corrected stories can be used with a different class to 'spot the differences' between the story they are given to read and the story the teacher reads to them aloud.

- Students write any story from scratch using different sensory systems.

*NB A fuller, multi-sensory version of the Asclepius story appeared in **In Your Hands**.*

PIRAEUS

Asclepius

Once Asclepius was walking in the countryside outside Athens when he met a traveller.

'Excuse me,' said the man, 'I'm going to Athens and I've never been there before. Have you any idea what it's like?'

'Where have you come from?' asked Asclepius.

'Piraeus,' said the traveller.

'Well what's that like?' asked Asclepius.

'Oh it's a dreadful place,' said the man.

'Well I expect you'll find Athens just the same,' said Asclepius.

'Oh dear,' said the man, and he went on his way.

A short time later, Asclepius met another traveller.

'Excuse me,' said the second man, 'I'm going to Athens and I've never been there before. Have you any idea what it's like?'

'Where have you come from?' asked Asclepius.

'Piraeus,' said the traveller.

'Well what's that like?' asked Asclepius.

'Oh it's a wonderful place,' said the man.

'Well I expect you'll find Athens just the same,' said Asclepius.

'Oh good,' said the man, and he went on his way.

ANSWERS TO ACTIVITY ON PAGE 89

Asclepius–father, Coronis–grandmother, Machaon–brother, Apollo–grandfather, Zeus–king of the gods, murderer of her grandmother

ASCLEPIUS REVISITED

Purpose

General interest; continuity.

Language focus

Quick reading (or listening) comprehension; family relationships.

PROCEDURE

♦ Tell students they will have only three minutes to read some information about Asclepius and then they will be asked some questions about the relationships between the different people. (Or prepare to read the information to them.)

♦ Give them the information face down, tell them all to turn over the paper together, and after three minutes, they turn the paper face down again.

♦ Give them the following question.

> In relation to Hygeia, who were:
> Asclepius? Coronis? Machaon? Apollo? Zeus?

Comment

This five-minute exercise can be used as a quick lesson filler at any appropriate time.

Apollo fell in love with a beautiful girl called Coronis, and she fell in love with him. But Apollo's raven told him that Coronis was also dallying with someone else. On hearing this news, Apollo, in a fit of jealousy, shot Coronis through the heart with his arrows.

Before her death, Coronis had had a son by Apollo, and this was Asclepius (also called Aesculapius). He was instructed by Apollo in the art of healing and became very good at it. In fact Asclepius' powers were so great that he could even bring the dead back to life. Zeus, the king of the gods, saw this and was extremely jealous of Asclepius so he hurled one of his thunderbolts at him and killed him.

Asclepius, father of the medical profession, handed down his medical knowledge and practice to his two sons, Machaon and Poladirius, and his daughter, Hygeia (who, of course, gave us the word 'hygiene').

Story telling for pronunciation

Story-telling can be an excellent vehicle for improving students' pronunciation. Good pronunciation is less about pronouncing individual sounds and more about good intonation. Everyone has good intonation in their own language, but for some reason, this often gets forgotten as they struggle to speak a new language 'correctly'. The most dramatic improvements in pronunciation can take place simply by practising story telling skills. The lesson sequence goes like this:

- The teacher tells the group that we are about to tell a story on to the tape. They should try to make the story as interesting and dramatic as possible.

- The students line up and read a line of a story each into a tape recorder. We then listen to the recorded story without comment – apart from the groans of the individuals concerned! It isn't necessary for the teacher to praise or criticise, everyone knows who has good pronunciation and who needs more work.

- The teacher does a quick comprehension check and students can ask for clarification of words or sentences they didn't understand.

- Students then stand in a different order. The teacher reads one line of the story at a time with good pronunciation. The student whose turn it is does the internal auditory monitoring (see page 37) and then repeats the line – several times, if necessary until they sound as near perfect as possible.

  The biggest problem is getting the students to slow down. 'Fluent' has often been interpreted to mean 'quick', which can lead to a great reduction in clarity. Story telling is meant to be slow, so that the listeners have time to hear, understand and enjoy the words.

- We practise making our voices sound warm and inviting as we walk around, each person reading the whole story aloud.

- The students stand in a different order again and read the story on to the tape, sentence by sentence, one student per sentence, concentrating on sounding warm and making it sound dramatic.

When Susan did this activity with a group of Italian teenagers, even though they all read a line which wasn't the one they had worked on with the teacher, the improvement was so dramatic that when we replayed the cassette, they burst into spontaneous applause – for themselves!

The second time she did the story-telling activity, the students knew what to expect and knew it could make a difference, so they approached it with great enthusiasm.

This time they worked in smaller groups on different stories, each with a cassette recorder. They started by practising the story themselves and recording it onto a cassette one line each. The teacher then gave each group a pre-recorded version of their story, and reminded them of the procedure, adding the element that they were totally responsible for their own learning. The one big reminder was to tell everybody to slow down, and to pay particular attention to the pauses and silences.

They listened to the story line by line, and coached one another on their pronunciation, following the internal auditory sequence. The teacher was there as a resource to answer questions if asked – mainly to check the understanding of a few expressions and to help with the pronunciation of sounds and words which were not totally clear on the tape. (This was also a wonderful chance for the teacher to sit back and just notice how the class interacted, how they helped one another – and they did – and particular aspects of pronunciation that individuals were good at and where they needed more help. The teacher also helped keep track of time – this phase took about 20-25 minutes.)

After the preparation time, the teacher reminded everybody that they were telling the story to a live audience, and to remember to make eye contact – and to take a deep breath before they started speaking. Each group told their story to the others, while the teacher recorded it onto cassette. At the end of each story (when the applause had died down) each group – including the tellers – took three minutes to give a grade out of ten for the pronunciation and the way the story was told and to pick out three things they had particularly liked. The tellers were much harder on themselves than the audience were and the feeling was of a job well done.

The teacher was also able to feed back on the story as a whole and on individual performances. Because of the observation time while students were preparing, it was possible to give precise praise to each individual, and to recommend to each student one thing they could do to improve their pronunciation. (The most frequent recommendations were to listen more carefully to native speaker models, to keep using the internal auditory monitoring, to slow down, to speak more clearly by opening their mouths and moving their lips, and to project their voices more – nothing about the 'th' sound or the difference between the long and short 'i', everything about clear communication, which is something within their control.)

By the way ... Many of the students borrowed the two recordings of 'their' story and made their own copy. This was not only a positive sign of their degree of involvement with the activity, but it boded well for their reading skills too. Research has shown that poor readers improve dramatically when they read along with a recording they themselves have made. Even though their own recording inevitably contains 'errors', they improve much more than if they read alongside a professional recording – presumably because of the motivation of it being personal to them. We should be aware of this 'personalisation' effect in many of our language learning activities.

Yes, but ...	Yes, and ...
These activities work with some of my students, but not all of them.	• Certain of your students will learn, regardless of what you do. Some may have problems which you will not be able to overcome within the realms of a normal teaching situation. *'If we had but world enough and time ...'* we believe that everyone could be helped to make the best of their potential. Most of our students can be helped to achieve more. • Make sure that you are using a range of activities that appeal to a range of different learners and that you are not simply choosing the activities which most appeal to you –presumably because they most fit your preferred learning styles. • Are you sure they're not working? Check with the specific students what their perception is. Ask them if there is anything you (and they) could do differently which would help them learn.

Belief

Belief is crucial. Someone once wrote that in order to be successful, you need to know what you want and you also need to believe that it's possible.

Your beliefs affect your life and the lives of those around you. What you believe about yourself determines what you do and don't do, what you're good at and what you're not good at. It determines your possibilities. What you believe about other people determines how you relate to them, how you behave with them and, therefore, how they respond to you.

Beliefs are like glasses: they cause us to see things in certain ways. (Consider the story of Asclepius on page 88.) This is not to say that what we believe is totally deterministic. Our beliefs don't necessarily make everything happen that we want to happen, but they do make it a lot more likely. And very often, believing that something is not possible means that we don't even have a go, so we never find out if it would have been possible or not.

Beliefs often become habits and it is not always easy to bring them to conscious awareness. Most of us are not used to examining our non-conscious motivations. When working with students, therefore, we find that it's often helpful to give some examples to get them started.

They are able who think they are able.

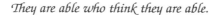

VIRGIL

BELIEVE IT OR NOT

Purpose

To investigate the power of belief.

Language focus

Reading/listening comprehension.

PROCEDURE

- Divide the class into two groups and give each group one of the stories (on a poster, or one copy for one student to read to the rest of the group, or one copy per student). Ask them to read the story and decide on a title or maybe more than one title. Possible titles might be: *The Man in the Refrigerator, Voodoo.*

- Rearrange the students into groups of four (or more), with at least two people from each of the original large groups in each of the new smaller groups.

- From the title(s), students try to guess what the other story is about. After three guesses each, they tell each other their stories.

- Students then discuss what the stories have in common and why they think each person died.

- Ask the class whether anyone knows any similar stories. You might also tell the story of Asclepius (page 88) and ask if it has anything in common with these two.

In 1964 a perfectly healthy man died of hypothermia. He was cleaning out a refrigeration truck when the door accidentally slammed shut. There was no-one else around and there was no way of opening the door from the inside. He knew that he wouldn't be found till the morning.

When he was found the next day, he was dead. He was stiff and cold, and his face and fingers were blue. He had clearly frozen to death.

And yet the extraordinary thing was that the electricity had actually been switched off. It had not been freezing in the refrigeration truck. It had not even been particularly cold. There was plenty of air, and there was no reason at all why he should have died.

A young woman in Haiti went out of her house one morning – and screamed. Her parents rushed out and found her, deathly pale, looking at something pinned to the door. It was a crudely-made wax doll, and the pin went straight into its heart. 'It's voodoo,' she whispered, as they tried to lift her up. 'I'm going to die.'

Her mother put her to bed, but she just lay there. She wouldn't speak, she wouldn't eat and she didn't seem to hear anything anyone said to her. Within a week she was dead.

Until the day she saw the wax doll, she had been healthy and happy, although she had recently ended a relationship with her boyfriend. The doctors could find no reason for her death.

FEARS

Purpose
Thinking about negative beliefs.

Language focus
Guessing vocabulary; narrative past tenses.

PROCEDURE

- Brainstorm the sorts of things people are often afraid of, eg heights, the dark, injections, the dentist, mice, spiders, snakes, flying, public speaking, exams, etc.

- (Optional) In pairs, students discuss the worksheet, using phrases such as:

    A *What do you think 'pnigophobia' means?*
    B *I'm not sure. I think it might be fear of choking.*
    A *So if I'm 'pnigophobic', I'm afraid of choking?*
    B *Yes, I think so.*

Fears

Match these expressions with their meaning.

1	xenophobia	means *fear of …*	a	beards
2	agoraphobia		b	the dark
3	claustrophobia		c	spiders
4	arachnaphobia		d	foreigners
5	hydrophobia		e	crowds
6	scotophobia		f	choking
7	paedophobia		g	being enclosed
8	pnigophobia		h	open spaces
9	pognophobia		i	water
10	demophobia		j	children

- Ask students to think individually of something they're afraid of. They should then think back to how they got to be afraid of that thing. What was the event or series of events that caused their fear?

- In small groups, they share their fears and describe the event(s) that caused them.

- Ask students to think individually if there has ever been any exception to this fear. If they are generally afraid of dogs, for example, has there ever been a dog that they weren't afraid of? Ask them to think – and then discuss in their group – what it was that made the difference for them not to be afraid.

- Students discuss situations when they were able to overcome their fear.

Comment

Offer students the option of keeping a fear secret. Ask them to join in the group discussion, either to help other people, or to discuss a fear they don't mind sharing, but ask them also to answer the questions for the activity in the privacy of their own heads about any 'secret' fears.

ANSWERS

1-d 2-h 3-g 4-c 5-i 6-b 7-j 8-f 9-a 10-e

CHILDHOOD STORIES

Purpose

Changing a story to alter its effect.

Language focus

Narrative present; *It made me realise/think about/doubt ...*

PROCEDURE

- ♦ Students think of a key story from their childhood: one that was read to them or one that they read to themselves frequently.

- ♦ In pairs, they tell their partner the story and then say what they particularly liked about it, eg the circumstances in which it was read, the story itself, the telling or reading of it, and so on.

- ♦ Students then discuss the effects – large or small, positive or negative – that this story has had on their life.

- ♦ Ask students to think about the following question: *'If you could change any parts of the story to make it an even better story and to enhance its positive effects on you (and minimise any negative ones), what bits would you change?'* Give them a moment to think individually about this before asking them to share their ideas with their partner. Partners can suggest ideas too.

- ♦ Students write a synopsis of their enhanced story (possibly for homework).

Comment

If students like their story just the way it is and don't want to change anything, that's fine. The exercise will nonetheless have raised their awareness of the story and of its effects on them.

Example

- ♦ Jane remembers a story called 'Jenny the Jeep'. It was about a lone pink jeep who is constantly taunted by the green jeeps who chant: 'Nasty little pink thing'. In the end an ice-cream seller comes to the jeep showroom looking for an ice-cream van and, of course, he chooses Jenny.

    Jane feels that the story brought out very strong feelings about injustice and fair play and is partly responsible for her anger in response to bullying or intolerance of any kind. She feels that toning down the story visually a bit (the faces of the green jeeps were cruel and evil), and cutting out some of the dreadful chanting, allows her to keep the message intact, but without the accompanying violent and aggressive feelings.

A belief is not merely an idea the mind possesses;
it is an idea that possesses the mind.

ROBERT BOLTON

Relax!

Research into the brain and studies on stress management both show that in order to look after ourselves properly and be at our best both physically and mentally, we need to pause from time to time and give our body and mind time to rest and recharge. Unless we do this, not only will we function less efficiently but we are in danger of allowing our stress levels to rise and of becoming over-tired and even ill.

It is difficult for students to concentrate for a whole hour at a time in the classroom. We need to give them moments when they can switch off and relax in order to apply themselves better in the next spurt of activity. These switching off moments also allow non-conscious processing to occur more effectively. Quick energisers (as described on pages 45-48) work well for this, and so do relaxation activities. They don't have to be very long and they make a lot of difference.

They get people into a good learning state and allow private time for re-focusing their concentration in a way appropriate to each individual.

Think calm

Have calm thoughts
Picture calm scenes
Recall calm sounds
And guess what you'll be feeling ...

Give yourself permission

Find a quiet place, regularly, and say out loud:
'For five minutes in every hour, I give myself
permission to relax and be calm.'
Keep repeating it to yourself

The Little Book of Calm Paul Wilson

SENSORY RELAXATION

Purpose
Relaxation, improving concentration.

Language focus
Shapes; textures; sounds; feelings.

PROCEDURE

♦ This relaxation exercise asks students first to concentrate on things external, and gradually to become more and more calm as they are encouraged to go inside. You can do any of the individual parts as a separate activity or you can do them one after another for a cumulative effect. We usually do the visual and auditory at one time, and the second kinaesthetic and pairwork activity (having reminded students of the first experience) on a subsequent occasion.

- **Shapes, colours and textures** Check or input basic vocabulary to do with shapes and textures – maybe just with a list on a poster. Ask students to take one minute to look around and notice not the objects in the room, but all the shapes, colours and textures that particularly catch their attention. They then tell a partner three things they have noticed particularly, possibly for the first time.

- **Peripheral vision** Ask students to take a deep breath and relax and then stare at a point at a distance in front of them. Without moving their eyes, they notice whatever else they can see in their peripheral vision. Get them to see things as far to their left and their right and as far above and below as they can. They can then compare their experience with a partner.

- **Sounds** Students sit quietly for one minute (eyes open or closed, as they wish) and notice how many different sounds they can hear. After a minute, ask students to call out all the things they could hear. Hopefully you will get lots of different sounds, ranging from the background hum of traffic in the far distance, sounds of other people or equipment in the building, and clocks and the shuffling of people in the room, to sounds within the body, such as breathing and swallowing. Add in things you heard too, and check any vocabulary.

  Then, having made everyone aware of most of the different sounds within earshot, ask students to relax and concentrate on the sounds around them. Listen first to the sounds far away in the distance … and then hear the sounds outside this building … then within the building outside this room … then the sounds within the room … the sounds very close to you … the sounds inside you … and then concentrate on the stillness and the silence at your centre, the source of your energy and well-being.

- **Feelings** Ask students to sit quietly and notice all the things they can feel, as in the previous sounds exercise. After about a minute, ask people to call out all the different things they can feel – the hardness of the chair I'm sitting on, the coolness of the air on my face, the feeling of my shirt on my arms, the tension in my neck, the tight feeling in my chest, etc. Then ask students to take a deep breath in and consciously relax each part of their body from the top of their head down to their toes.

- **Pairwork** Students work in pairs, sitting very close together so that they can hear each other if they talk in quiet voices, but also in a position where they can relax. One person starts by saying something they can see, eg *I can see the light coming in through the window.* The other person acknowledges that and adds something they can hear, eg *You can see the light coming in through the window and I can hear birds singing outside.* The first person adds something they can feel, eg *You can hear birds singing outside and I can feel the warmth of my hands on my lap.* They continue adding things they can see, hear and feel, always acknowledging the thing the person said immediately before them. The cumulative effect is very calming and relaxing. (This (in)activity is also a very effective way of relaxing on one's own.)

IMAGE STREAMING

Purpose

Enhancing internal visual skills; building class rapport; increasing concentration.

Language focus

Fluency; listening comprehension; description in the present.

PROCEDURE

- Demonstrate the activity with a fairly confident student. Sit opposite each other, with heads fairly close together so you can talk quietly to one another (but in the demonstration speak loudly enough for everyone to hear).

  Start by describing something you can see in your head, Your partner tries to see what you are describing. After a short time, you stop speaking and they carry on describing how the scene is developing for them. You follow what they say. Continue taking turns describing the scene.

  An example dialogue might begin:

A *I can't really see anything. Just sort of black. Well, reddish black. Oh, now there are some clouds. White fluffy clouds in a blue sky. Can you see them?*

B *Er, no. Yes. Very small white clouds, high in the sky. The sun's shining. It's a very hot day. I'm standing in a big green field, looking up.*

A *Yes, and the grass is quite long. I can feel it on my legs. I've got bare feet. There are lots of flowers in the field. Yellow and red.*

B *And some small blue flowers. I can smell the grass. I want to sit down. Actually, I want to lie down. My hands are under my head. I'm looking up, high into the sky.*

A *I feel as if I'm floating. I'm floating up into the sky. I'm flying through the clouds. My arms are stretched out and I'm flying. High above the ground. Down below, I can see green fields and a few houses and some people. They're very very small. I feel really free.*

- Before students try the activity in pairs, answer any questions and suggest that they describe sounds, feelings and smells as well as pictures. Remind them that they are trying to imagine as closely as possible the same thing, and both have the chance to influence the direction of the fantasy.

- Students do the activity with a partner. You might have classical or New Age music playing quietly in the background to allow greater privacy.

- Students discuss the experience with their partner and then feed back to the class any important impressions or insights they have had.

Grammar

The NLP view of language is complex, particular and fascinating. It provides an alternative to the standard grammar book definitions of the use of specific tenses. For language teaching purposes, the important thing is to concentrate first on the meaning of what people are actually saying – and then to relax and have fun with the language.

NLP as such does not suggest a method of teaching language. However NLP beliefs and techniques can be incorporated into almost any approach to language teaching. Our own view is that it is not necessary to follow a strict structural order when teaching language. You may need to follow a coursebook or an imposed syllabus, but sometimes add in some of the freer, more individual tasks, where the motivation provided by the language content compensates for a potentially higher language level. We find that students frequently ask for grammatical explanations or help – which is when it is very easy to input whatever is required.

The 'presentation – practice – free stage' model of inputting new language is already well known and we are not going to repeat it here. We would like to suggest that sometimes you take an alternative approach and give unstructured meaningful input, eg taking a topical news item or a personal anecdote, where the content provides the stimulus to understanding.

This section presents a variety of exercises which will hopefully encourage you and students to take a fresh look at language. It also gives ways of maximising students' potential to learn language with the minimum of effort.

Peripheral awareness   Make use of students' peripheral awareness to enhance non-conscious learning. Prepare examples of the target language area, eg newspaper headlines, stories, poems and jokes. Stick them up round the walls well before you start introducing the structure actively. At the appropriate time (perhaps dictated by the coursebook), use one of your normal methods to introduce and practise the language. As you gather information, students' work, grammatical explanations from other books and so on, add them to the wall display

Leave the material up for some time after the specific input and practice is finished. After a week or two, use the material as the basis of a revision quiz. Give the students warning before you take down the material so they have private review time and a chance to copy down anything they think is particularly memorable for them (we find it profitable to allow class time for this). Students quickly become used to this system and often start looking consciously at the material – which has to be a bonus!

Overview   Take a longish text in English at any level, eg a newspaper article. Give students some aspects of language you feel is at their level or slightly above, eg present tenses, plurals, adjectives, ways of referring to the future, phrasal verbs, suggestions, etc. Ask them to scan through the text and underline or highlight examples of such language.

Purpose

To help students become aware at a feeling level of the conceptual meaning of a grammatical structure.

Language focus and preparation

Revision of the present perfect (or any grammatical structure).

PROCEDURE

♦ Quickly check that students understand the vocabulary in the example sentences, plus the words *smell, taste, chew, swallow, bite, lick.*

♦ Tell students you are going to guide them on an inner grammatical experience as you eat a biscuit. Check that everyone is happy to eat a biscuit – in their minds. (If you have resistance, you can change the biscuit to a piece of fruit – or suggest that students can have the pleasure of eating a biscuit even if it is not something they would normally do – it's only in their mind, after all.) Ask students to relax and go inside. Then lead them through a guided fantasy.

Imagine a biscuit. A delicious biscuit. The sort you really like. Pick it up and look at it closely. Notice how crisp and fresh it is. Smell it. Notice how your mouth is beginning to water. In a moment you are going to eat the biscuit. Say the words to yourself: 'I am going to eat this biscuit.'

Hold the biscuit close to your nose and mouth for a moment. Wait. Think how delicious it will taste. And then, slowly, bite into it. Slowly chew the biscuit and notice how delicious it tastes on your tongue and in your mouth. You're eating a biscuit. Say the words to yourself: 'I'm eating a biscuit.' 'I'm really enjoying this biscuit.'

Keep the biscuit in your mouth for a moment longer ... and then swallow. Take another bite. Chew it. Taste it. Enjoy it. Now put the rest of the biscuit into your mouth. As you chew, say to yourself again: 'I'm eating a biscuit.' 'I'm really enjoying this biscuit.' And then swallow. Lick your lips, move your tongue all around the inside of your mouth to catch any last little bits of biscuit and swallow them.

Notice how you feel now. Notice the taste in your mouth. Notice how your stomach feels with a biscuit inside it. Notice how you feel emotionally. You have eaten a biscuit. Say the words to yourself: 'I've eaten a biscuit.'

How are you feeling? Think of the words to describe how you're feeling now. Take a deep breath in and gently come back to the room, bringing the feeling with you. Open your eyes.

- Ask students to describe how they are feeling now – the feeling of the present perfect. Listen for any statements which link the past (eating the biscuit) with the present feeling (eg *I feel full. I feel a bit guilty. I'm not hungry any more. I've got a nice taste in my mouth. I feel fat.*) Ask them to say again the sentence which describes why they feel this: '*I've eaten a biscuit*'.

- Put a large piece of paper on the wall and write at the top, '*I've eaten a biscuit.*' Ask students to write what they feel now underneath.

- On other pieces of paper, write sentences such as: *I've painted a picture. I've swum across the lake. I've just been for a walk. I've had a row with my boy/girlfriend. I've finished my homework. I've cleaned my teeth.* Ask students to stand in front of each sentence, close their eyes and strongly imagine what they have done in order to be saying that sentence now. Then they write on the paper how they feel now.

- Leave the papers on the wall until the next lesson (or longer) as a reminder of the feeling link to the grammatical structure.

Follow up

- In the following lesson, you can contrast the feeling of the present perfect with the past simple. Look quickly at all the papers on the wall (having put them up again if you had to take them down). Ask students to remember that they did these things in the last lesson. Ask them to close their eyes and notice how they are feeling now. Then ask them to contrast this feeling with the feeling they remember from the last lesson. Ask them to say the sentence to themselves: '*Last Tuesday I ate a biscuit*'. Discuss the comparison between the feelings. (I can remember the taste, but I can't actually taste it. I felt full but now I'm hungry.) Similarly elicit sentences and feelings relating to the other sentences, eg '*On Tuesday I went for a walk*'. Then I felt happy and exhilarated and a bit tired. Now I'm feeling that I need some exercise'.

Variations

- Having done the exercise fully once, you can do a similar 'journey' to exemplify other tenses. Make sure you use a very different example, so that students can clearly differentiate between the different tenses. Make sure that students state the example sentence clearly to themselves at a peak point in the experience.

- You can also do this exercise to present a tense for the first time.

Comment

Everyone is entitled to feel what they feel, but make sure that the feelings students express are consistent with the use of the tense as used by a native speaker. The key is to make sure that the experience you describe is totally consistent with the use of the tense in the target language.

REVIEW OF TENSES

Purpose

To help students become aware at a feeling level of the conceptual meaning of grammatical structures.

Language focus and preparation

Revision of a range of structures. Students should already have met the form and meaning of the example sentences.

This exercise is much more effective if students have previously experienced a fully guided 'Inner Grammar' exercise (see previous pages).

PROCEDURE

- Ask students to go inside and experience fully each sentence as you say it. They say the sentence several times to themselves inside their heads and notice how they are feeling. Then they open their eyes and discuss their feelings.

- Compare the feelings they get with a variety of different tenses. You say the example sentence, students go inside and notice how they feel when they say the sentences several times to themselves. They then open their eyes and discuss the feelings. Experiment with sentences such as the following:

I'm eating a biscuit.

I've eaten a biscuit.

I ate a biscuit.

I eat biscuits.

I don't eat biscuits.

I'm going to eat a biscuit.

I'm hungry. I think I'll eat a biscuit.

I wish I hadn't eaten the biscuit.

I like biscuits.

I don't like biscuits.

I really like biscuits.

I really don't like biscuits.

I don't really like biscuits.

I ate the last biscuit.

I had just eaten the last biscuit, when my friend came in.

I was eating the last biscuit when my friend came in.

My friend came in, so I didn't eat the last biscuit.

If my friend hadn't come in, I would have eaten the biscuit.

If my friend had come in, I wouldn't have eaten the biscuit.

The dog bit the cat.

My dog bit the cat.

The cat was bitten by a dog.

My cat was bitten by your dog

Comment

Start with simple sentences. Link sentences with one another, so students experience the contrast. Make sure your tone of voice gives a clear indication of the meaning of the sentences.

This is a revision exercise. Students should already know (or have previously encountered) the different tenses — they cannot experience something they don't understand.

Timelines

Timelines in NLP are not the relationships between the tenses in a grammar book. They are an excellent way to help people clarify their goals, access useful memories and link the past, the present and the future in positive ways. However, one should tread carefully. Although most people are quite happy to think about their past and their future and to notice how their mind works, occasionally we come across someone who does not want to do this kind of activity. We always respect their right to opt out. We ask them to do the activity about an invented person – preferably someone of their own age, but of the opposite sex living in a totally different situation. In this way, they can take part in the language activity, with much less risk of stirring up memories you and they do not want to deal with in the classroom.

Note also that all the activities concentrate very much on *positive* experiences.

INNER TIMELINES

Purpose
To help students become aware of their own inner concept of time.

Language focus
Listening comprehension; prepositions of place (in the discussion).

PROCEDURE

- Prepare students for this activity by asking them consciously to list five or six good memories from their past and three or four good things they can imagine happening to them in the future. If appropriate, they can share their ideas with a partner.

- Ask students to sit comfortably, relax and go inside. Ask them to follow your words, making pictures in their minds. When you ask them to point, you mean physically to point with their fingers. Some people might get very clear pictures, others might get rather smudgy pictures, but all should be able to point to where those pictures are. Explain that people often 'store' pictures of the future and the past in different places in their minds, usually on a sort of line. The purpose of this exercise is to find out how they store time in their minds.

> *Picture yourself sitting where you are in your chair. And now imagine yourself at the end of today, getting ready to go to bed tonight. Notice where you can see that future picture in your mind. Point to that picture.*

- Ask students to keep pointing and open their eyes to see where other people are pointing. (In between making different time pictures, students may open their eyes to see where other students are pointing if they want to. Ask them not to comment until the end of the exercise. Remind them that there are no right or wrong ways of storing time.)

Close your eyes, go inside, and remember something really nice that happened yesterday. Make a picture of it in your mind. Point to the picture.

Remember something really good that happened last week. Picture it in your mind. Point to the picture. Where is it in relation to the previous picture?

Remember something special that happened last year. Make a picture of it in your mind. Point to the picture.

Remember something fantastic that happened when you were a small child of about five or six. Make a picture of it in your mind. Point to the picture.

Gently, come to the present time again and feel yourself sitting in your chair in this room. Point to the picture of yourself sitting comfortably in your chair now. Open your eyes and look around. Point to the line from now going into the past. Compare your past timeline with other people's.

Close your eyes again, go inside, and imagine enjoying yourself next weekend. Make a clear picture. Where is it in relation to the previous picture? Point to it.

Think about yourself leaving school having passed your final exam. Make a picture of yourself being congratulated by your school friends. Point to it.

Imagine yourself ten years in the future. You have a job. Imagine yourself feeling fulfilled and happy as you set out to go to work in the morning. Point to the picture of yourself ten years in the future.

Imagine yourself as a very old person, still fit and well. It is your birthday. Imagine yourself sitting in a comfortable chair, with friends and family all around, wishing you a happy birthday. Point to that picture well into the future.

Come back to the present and feel yourself sitting in your chair. Point to the picture of yourself sitting comfortably in your chair now.

Open your eyes and point to your timeline, past, present and future. Compare with other people your inner concept of time.

Comments

Although there are no right or wrong ways of storing time, some ways are more helpful than others, and it is possible to change timelines. (If you don't like the change, you can always put it back to the way it was.) For example, some people store the future behind them, and find it difficult to 'look forward' to things. Suggest that they turn round. Some people store different parts of the future in lots of different places, so they might find it easier to see a 'clear direction in which they want to go' if they move the different parts onto a more defined line. Some people are not on their time line now, and feel a bit distant from what is going on around them. Ask them to try stepping onto their line.

Once you have given a few examples, and people have seen how others experience time, people can try out different timelines and make changes which seem more useful to them. Discussing the possibilities can be a fascinating source of language practice

The future part of this particular exercise has been written for, and used with, groups of school pupils. It will obviously need adapting if you intend to use it with adult learners, eg 'Think about yourself in a year's (ten years' ...) time doing some of the things that you really want to do, feeling fulfilled and happy,' and so on.

Purpose

To help students become aware at a feeling level of the link between time and grammatical structures.

Language focus and preparation

Revision of a range of structures. Students should already have met the form and meaning of the example sentences.

This exercise is much more effective if students have previously established their own 'timeline' with the preceding exercise. Before they start the exercise, ask them to point to their timeline, past, present and future.

PROCEDURE

♦ Explain that as you say sentences in different tenses, students should make a picture (or pictures) of what you say. They can notice the time the picture relates to and the place in their minds where they see the picture. They point to the picture.

♦ Ask students to sit comfortably, relax and go inside. They say the following sentences (or your own variations to suit the age and experience of your students). After each sentence, students open their eyes and compare where they are pointing. Remember that different people may well have different concepts of time, so they can explain to one another where they are pointing in relation to the time they can 'see' in their mind's eye.

I'm sitting in a chair here and now.

I'm watching my favourite TV programme.

I've been watching videos all day.

I've watched four videos today.

I was watching a video when the phone rang …

It was some really exciting news.

Earlier today I smelled something burning …

I found the iron left on, burning a hole in my best shirt …

So I switched it off and put the shirt in the sink.

I've got to buy a new shirt tomorrow.

I've got something special to do next week.

I've never liked camping.

I've always liked camping.

Yesterday I went to my favourite place and had a wonderful time.

Last year I ate pizza 10 times.

I've always liked chocolate.

When I was a child, I didn't like cabbage.

I've been learning English for several years.

I used to go to primary school.

Now I go to secondary school..

Comment

It will not be easy to place every sentence in a particular place, but the discussion of where people feel they want to put the sentences should lead to an interesting discussion about the relationship between tenses and time.

REVISING ON A TIMELINE

Purpose

Revision.

Language focus

All recently learnt language.

PROCEDURE

♦ Demonstrate with a volunteer. You read the instructions, they carry them out. (The timeline need not match students' own internal representation of time.)

> *Imagine a line on the floor going to the past in one direction and to the future in the other. The middle of the line is now, the present. Knowing everything you know now, step onto the line, in the present, and walk slowly into the past to the beginning of (the learning period)*. As you go, with all your new knowledge, remember all the different things you have learnt.*
>
> *When you get back to the beginning, remember the moment when you walked into the classroom and sat down. Turn round and look forward to the present, noticing how far you will travel. With your new knowing eyes, look at all the activities and learning you will do.*
>
> *Then walk towards the present, picking up any bits and pieces of learning that you didn't notice on the way down. When you reach the present, look once more back into the past and be aware of all the things you have learnt, and feel proud of yourself.*
>
> *Now turn and look to the future and realise how all the things you have learnt so far are going to make it so easy for you to continue learning tomorrow, and next week and next year, and well into your future. Walk into the future as far as you want to and experience that sense of easy and successful learning. Turn around, look back and appreciate how far you have come. When you're ready walk back to the present and standing here, now, have a real sense of present, past and future learning. When you're ready, step off and come gently back to the room and to the here and now.*
>
> • *Say 'this lesson', 'this week', 'this term','this course', or whatever learning period you use.*

♦ Students work in pairs. One student reads the instructions to the other, who does the activity. Then they change places.

♦ Students share their experience with their partner and exchange their personal key learnings.

♦ Group discussion. How far were the things people learnt part of a shared experience, and how much of what they learnt was individual to them?

Variation

♦ Students can do this activity in their heads, sitting quietly in their seats. With all the knowledge they have now, they go back to the moment when they came into the classroom and sat down … and they relive the course, noticing everything they did and all the things they learnt, and all the things they found difficult at first, but which they now find easy. And they bring all this learning back to the present and feel very proud of everything they have learnt.

Modelling

One good way of achieving your goals is to copy or 'model' people who can do things you would like to do, or have skills you would like to have. If you want to be a good skier, model the best skiers. If you want to be a good student, model the best students you know.

How do you model someone? The first thing is to observe them very carefully, and notice what they do. Then you can 'second-position' them (see page 127): imagine what it's like to be in their skin doing what they do in the way that they do it. The essential bit, though, is to think as they think, and it is not always easy to know how they think – very often they don't know themselves, that's 'just how they are'.

People have strategies for doing things. Some of these are conscious (eg Susan always sets her alarm ten minutes early, so that she can have a few minutes to wake up gently in the mornings), but many are non-conscious. It is possible to think about the internal strategies people have for doing things. They usually consist of making internal pictures, hearing internal sounds or voices (often talking to yourself), and checking how you feel, in some regular sequence. For example, when the time actually comes for Susan to get out of bed, she gets a tight feeling in her stomach and then sees a picture of herself standing up by the bedroom door. On warm days, or days when something nice – or urgent – is happening, she says something like, *'OK then'* to herself, and gets up. On cold days, or when she's tired, she can follow the 'feeling/picture' sequence three or four times, with the tight feeling in her stomach getting stronger each time, until eventually she says the words in a resigned tone of voice – and gets out of bed. This is not a particularly efficient strategy – not one that you would want to learn – and it would be possible to refine it so that she didn't have the bad feeling in her stomach, but since it gets her up on time, she hasn't bothered to change it.

Modelling is a basic tenet of NLP, as well as having been its starting point, so although it might take a bit of practice, it is worth giving students at least an awareness of how it might be used.

When you are learning skills and strategies from another person, you only want to take on their strengths, not their weaknesses. Choose your people to model carefully. Only model those aspects of their behaviour which you want to make your own. Before you start, clearly ask your non-conscious mind to protect you. It will.

Someone who can copy can do.

LEONARDO DA VINCI

Purpose

Helping students focus on aspects of communication other than the words spoken.

Language focus

Phatic communication.

PROCEDURE

- Show students any short video of native speakers of English interacting in some way, preferably moving around. Give students the worksheet and ask them to read through all the questions. Ask half the class to look for the body language and the other half to listen for verbal language (or you could allocate just one or two things for each person – or pair – to look or listen for). Everyone can answer the question, *'What other things do you notice?'* Students then watch the video and write down anything they notice about the way the people on the video behave, compared to the way people behave in their own culture.

- In groups of four or five, students compare their notes so far.

- Watch the video again with the sound turned down, so that everyone can concentrate on visual cues. In their groups, students compare notes.

- Watch the video a third time asking students to listen specifically to the sound of the voices, rather than the words. Students compare notes.

- Watch the video in black and white. Students might notice different things.

- Ask students to sit with four new people and compare notes.

- With the whole class, discuss the main differences between the people on the video and people of the students' culture(s) in a similar situation. Identify the things you could copy if you want to speak more like a native speaker.

Comment

You might raise the question of over-generalising and stereotyping. Not all native speakers are the same. Some things students notice on the video may be due to the social situation, or the age and sex of the people. However, there are probably certain tendencies which are noticeably characteristic of cultures and which can be approximated.

Yes, but...	*Yes, and...*
Isn't this manipulation?	... so it is! And so are many of the things teachers do in classrooms. We are manipulating students into positions they would not have adopted on their own, in order to help them learn new things. However, we do it openly and explain to them what we are doing and why. Manipulation is a negative word. We prefer to call it helping. It is also true that the more we help people understand how they can be manipulated, the more likely they are to recognise manipulation when it comes from less benign sources and be able to counter it effectively.

NATIVE SPEAKER WATCHING

Watch the video and make notes about the way the native speakers interact with one another. Notice both the things which are the same as in your culture and the things which are different.

What facial expressions do they use?

Do they make eye contact? How often?

What do you notice about their mouth movements?

Do they use gestures with their hands? What sort? How big? How often?

How are they standing or sitting or moving?

How close are they to one another?

Do they touch one another? How? Where?

How loudly do they speak?

How fast?

What do you notice about the rhythm of their speech?

And their intonation patterns?

What noises do they make which are not actual words?

What other things do you notice?

Purpose

Helping students improve their awareness of and competence in communicating in the target language.

Language focus

Phatic communication; listening; fluency; pronunciation.

PROCEDURE

You might like to do some or all of these steps:

- Choose a short section (one or two minutes) of a video for students to copy exactly. Show the video once and check basic comprehension.

- Turn the sound off and play the video again, asking students to notice particularly the character's gestures.

- Everyone stands up, and as you play the video again (without sound), everyone (including the teacher) copies the character's gestures, at the same time as the character (in reality everyone is bound to be slightly behind the character). Acknowledge that people might feel a bit embarrassed and therefore laugh, exaggerate or not do it very well the first time. Keep going with good humour.

- Play the video again, this time asking students to listen to the 'music' of the way the character talks. Play one phrase at a time for everyone to imitate the stress, rhythm, and rise and fall of the voice, while repeating the syllable 'la'.

- Once you have been through the whole section, play the video again, with the sound turned low, while everyone copies the gestures and voice of the character (still saying 'la' instead of words).

- Give students a script of the words, or ask them to do a (gapped) dictation. By now students already have an idea of the meaning of the communication.

- Play the video a phrase or sentence at a time for everyone to copy, saying the actual words this time. Then play the whole sequence through with everyone copying the character exactly, with the actual words. You might do this as echo listening (see page 36).

- Ask all the students to practise acting out the role, as if they are the character. Everyone practises at once. They can look at their copy of the words, but should not be reading aloud.

- Finally, play the video again with the sound turned down and everyone acts along with the character.

Comment

The choice of video is quite important. Make sure the character is someone appropriate for students to copy. Not all teenagers want to imitate an elderly professor, for example.

Follow up

- Tell students they are about to have fun being native speakers of English. Ask them to walk around the room, moving like a native speaker and doing the things they have observed in terms of body language. From time to time they should stop and have a brief chat with other people (*Hello. How are you? Nice day. How's your father?* etc), in role as a native speaker.

Purpose

To help students become aware that their minds work in different ways.

Language focus

Numbers; calculations; countries; listening; fluency.

PROCEDURE

♦ Tell students you are going to give them some puzzles. Their first task is to solve the puzzles. Their second task is to notice how their minds work and whether they work differently for different puzzles, and differently from other people's minds. They write down the answers and notice the process they go through mentally to work out each one. They must not shout out the answers, because that stops everyone else thinking. They remain silent and put up their hand when they've finished, so they know you know that they know – if you know what we mean!

♦ Stop after each group of puzzles, check the answers, and discuss how students found their answers. Elicit as many different strategies from students as possible. Note them on the board.

♦ After doing as many puzzles as you think appropriate, ask students whether they are aware of strategies other people use which they themselves don't usually use. Point out that if they use a lot of different strategies when solving puzzles and problems in the future, they are more likely to come up with solutions.

Comment

Do the puzzles one group at a time and keep them in the control of the teacher. If you give them all out at once, students simply dash for the solutions, rather than noticing their mental strategies. We recommend dictating the maths problems in order to slow the students down a bit.

Do as many or as few of these puzzles as you (and the students) like. You can probably find lots more which generate extra language work for odd periods at the beginning and end of lessons. Encourage students to bring in different sorts of puzzles too.

——— Answers and comments on the puzzles (pages 112-113) ———

Group 1 – Spatial puzzles

Country capitals

One of the things students probably did was stop looking for other answers once they'd found the first. Students who are able to solve this problem quickly usually visualise a map and move around it counting out the names of the countries and capitals, often physically counting on their fingers. Suggest that students try visualising problems to make them real – they will find it easier if they look up inside their heads.

Answers 1-Austria, Ireland or Germany 2-Bolivia or Ecuador

Join the dots

The answer involves breaking out of the assumed limitation of the imaginary box created by the dots. If someone already knows it (or when someone works out the answer), ask them to join the dots with fewer than four straight lines without taking their pen off the paper. (You could use a very thick pen to cover all nine dots at once; you could roll the paper into a cylinder and keep drawing round the paper until you've connected all the dots with one continuous line; you could draw a line twice round the globe, connecting a line of dots each time, etc.)

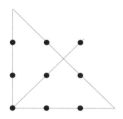

Country capitals

1 It's a country with seven letters. It's in Europe, but it isn't one of the countries in the UK. There are six letters in the name of its capital (in English). Which country is it?

2 It's a country with seven letters. It's in Latin America. There are five letters in the name of its capital. Which country is it?

Join the dots

Join these nine dots with four straight lines without taking your pen off the paper.

Calculations

a) Multiply 2 by 3.

b) Multiply 6 by 7.

c) Multiply 7 by 6.

d) Multiply 23 by 10.

e) Multiply 11 by 12.

f) Multiply 23 by 13.

g) Subtract 2 from 4.

h) Subtract 10 from 20.

i) Subtract 9 from 23.

j) Subtract 68 from 123.

What does Paul like?

If Fred likes photography, coughing, laughter, toffee and fun, and he hates pictures, captains, tea, tears and spaghetti bolognaise, what does Paul like?

Forwards, backwards and upside-down

Can you think of a word in English which, when written in capital letters, reads the same forwards, backwards and upside-down?

(You might find this easier if you think about it around midday.)

Odd-one-out

Which is the odd-one-out in each set? Why?

1	coughed	laughed	taught	sighed	ploughed
2	song	tune	piano	music	concert
3	happy	Sunday	wonderfully	lovely	nice
4	coffee	banana	cheese	apple	peer
5	one	two	four	six	ten

Group 4

The chicken, the fox and the corn.

A farmer wanted to cross a river with a chicken, a fox and some corn. He could only carry one of them at one time, but he couldn't leave the fox alone with the chicken (the fox would eat the chicken) or the chicken alone with the corn (the chicken would eat the corn). How did he get himself and everything else across the river?

Cockerel on a roof

A cockerel is sitting exactly in the middle of a roof which has one slope at 33% and the other slope at 45%. It lays an egg exactly at the top at the point where the two slopes meet. Where will the egg go?

Rising tide

A ladder with twelve rungs is hanging over the side of a boat. Its rungs are exactly 30 cms apart and two are under water. The tide is rising at the rate of 15 cms an hour. After three hours, how many rungs will be under water?

Group 5

Triangles

How many triangles are there in this figure?

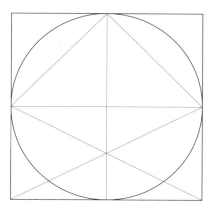

Symbols

What is the next symbol in this sequence?

Group 2 – Mathematical puzzles

Calculations

Students probably noticed a big difference between the calculations they 'knew automatically', the calculations they knew if they thought about it (eg because they knew their tables by heart), and ones they had to work out, either in their heads or on paper – or the ones they copied from other people!

Answers a-6   b-42   c-42   d-230   e-132   f-299   g-2   h-10   i-14   j-55

Group 3 – Linguistic puzzles

What does Paul like?

If students cannot work out the answer, offer them the following example as an extra clue: Susan likes psychology, her ceiling, singing, whistling and toast with syrup. She hates her floor, therapy, talking, humming and bread with jam.

Answers Fred only likes words containing the sound 'f', the first letter of his name. We assume that Paul likes anything containing the sound 'p', eg captains, pictures, and he loves pepper.

Forwards, backwards and upside-down
Answer NOON

Odd-one-out

You may find other reasons than those give here. If so, that's excellent!

Answers 1 taught is irregular   2 music is uncountable   3 nice doesn't end in y; Sunday is spelt with a capital letter   4 peer is not food; banana isn't spelt with a double letter   5 one is an odd number, the others are even; four has four letters, the others have three.

Group 4 – Lateral thinking puzzles

The chicken, the fox and the corn
Answer The farmer rowed across the river with the chicken, leaving the fox and the corn behind. He rowed back with an empty boat. He took across the fox, leaving the corn behind. At the far side, he left the fox, but took back the chicken. At the first bank, he left the chicken and took the corn across. He left the fox with the corn and went back to fetch the chicken.

Cockerel on a roof
Answer Probably to a laboratory or a museum: it would be the first cockerel ever to lay an egg!

Rising tide
Answer Still two; the boat will rise with the tide.

Group 5 – Visual puzzles

Symbols
Answer The symbols are made by writing numbers with their mirror image.

Triangles
Answer 19

BEING AN A1 TEACHER

Purpose

Making students aware of the skills of teaching and learning.

Language focus

Present simple; adjectives.

PROCEDURE

- Students think of excellent teachers they have had in their lives and write down five to ten qualities or things they did which made them excellent.
- Students do the same for 'bad' teachers.
- Ask them to check back and see which teachers helped them learn most. (We tend to mark teachers as 'excellent' if we liked them and 'bad' if we didn't, but sometimes we can learn a lot from people we don't necessarily like.)
- Ask students to share their ideas in small groups. Then their task is to agree on and write a list of the ten qualities which make up their 'ideal teacher'.
- Students walk round and look at all the other lists.
- Class discussion about 'being a good teacher'.

Comment

You, the teacher, might like to do this exercise for yourself. Measure yourself against your own criteria, find things you could do to improve your teaching, and put them into practice immediately.

Do this exercise before doing the 'A1 student' exercise which follows. By focusing on the teacher, students are likely to be more honest and less defensive, while still thinking about conditions which help them learn.

BEING AN A1 STUDENT

Purpose

Making students aware of learning strategies.

Language focus

Present simple; adjectives; *should*; *going to.*

PROCEDURE

- Follow the procedure for 'being an A1 teacher', with students thinking about 'good' and 'bad' students they have known.
- Students produce a checklist for new students to the school: 'How to be an A1 student', using *'You should/shouldn't ...'*
- Students then evaluate themselves against the checklist and determine three things they could do to become better students.
- Everyone stands up, and altogether (so nobody can actually hear anyone else) they make three statements about what they are going to do to be a better student, using *'I'm going to ...'*

TRANSFERRING STRATEGIES

Purpose

Improving learning strategies.

Language focus

Present simple; sequencing.

PROCEDURE

- Students think about their strategies for doing homework or their attitude to washing up or working in their least favourite lesson – whichever they dislike more! What is their attitude? When do they do it? How do they feel about doing homework or cleaning the house or filing? What is it that finally makes them get started? How do they feel when they've finished? What comments do teachers, colleagues or family members make to them about their work and their attitude to work? (Most people could do with some improvement in this area.)

- Students then think about their attitude to something they enjoy but which involves skill and which they have to work at or train for in their leisure time. It must be something they enjoy (ie not something forced on them by parents or the pressures of their job), such as playing a sport for a team, playing an instrument, sewing, cooking, practising martial arts, drawing, painting, etc. If nothing fits this category, then ask them to imagine themselves getting ready for something they really want to do, such as going out with friends.

- Students write down their strategy for the activity they enjoy. What do they think? What do they do?

- Give students the homework/football examples (see next page) to read in groups and compare with their own and their colleagues' strategies.

- Students think again about their own strategies and add any further stages they have thought of as a result of seeing what other people do (it isn't always easy to work out what exactly it is that we do).

- Students who think their work strategy could do with some improvement should imagine applying their leisure activity strategy to their work.

- Discuss anything students have learnt. Ask for a commitment to try the strategy.

Modelling pronunciation

Sometimes students are concentrating so much on the pronunciation they think is right, that they don't listen to what they actually hear. Caricature and exaggeration focus on the main differences between the native and non-native speaker pronunciation. Ask students to try the following:

- Mimic someone of your own nationality speaking English. Really exaggerate! If you know what you're exaggerating, you also know the things to work on.

- Mimic an English person speaking your language. Really exaggerate again! Notice what you are exaggerating and realise that the 'mistakes' an English person makes are carried over from English pronunciation.

- Mimic an English person speaking English. Really exaggerate! Good, isn't it?

STRATEGIES

HOMEWORK

As soon as I get home, I dump my schoolbag on the floor and forget about it.

I do anything and everything except my homework, even when I haven't really got anything to do.

I have a bad feeling in my stomach because I know I've got to do my homework.

I avoid my parents so that they don't ask me about my homework.

Eventually my mum tells me to do my homework.

I get everything out of my bag onto the table and sit and look at it. I put on my favourite music and listen to it. If my mum comes in, I pretend to be working.

Eventually I imagine myself going to school the next day without having done my homework. I get a heavy feeling in my chest and feel bad. I say to myself 'You'd better get on with it then.' I sigh and feel bad. I start working without any enthusiasm. Once I've started, I usually find it isn't too bad and that I can do it quite well, and I wish I hadn't wasted all that time feeling bad.

I do this every time!

FOOTBALL PRACTICE

I put all my kit into the wash as soon as I get back from practice, so that it's ready for next time.

I look forward to football practice all week and imagine myself being picked for the team. I imagine how I'll feel. I see myself having possession of the ball, running towards the goal and scoring. I hear people shouting my name and encouraging me. I imagine myself scoring the winning goal, and I hear everyone yelling. I feel great every time I think about it. It's my favourite fantasy.

On practice days, my mates and I always get there and get changed early and we go out and get warmed up and kick the ball around a bit before the coach comes out. We help each other with things we're good at and they help us where we need practice, and there's quite a bit of good-natured competition and we have a good laugh.

When the coach comes out, we stop messing about. We do exactly what he says, even when it's hard, because if you don't he doesn't pick you for the team. I keep practising really hard, even when he's not watching me, because I know that it's making me a better player.

When the practice is over, I really enjoy the atmosphere in the changing rooms and we're all still talking about the game and the things we did and how we can get better. I love it.

How about watching a video with the class on the theme of being a 'good' teacher, eg *Dead Poets Society, To Sir With Love, Mr Holland's Opus, Dangerous Minds* – or even *Good Will Hunting*. Have a follow-up discussion in the light of their learning from the exercises on being an A1 teacher and student (see page 115).

Purpose

To help students become aware of their strengths as learners of English, and to give students new strategies for learning.

Language focus

Describing strategies; *good at -ing*.

PROCEDURE

♦ Brainstorm all the different aspects of learning and using a new language, eg

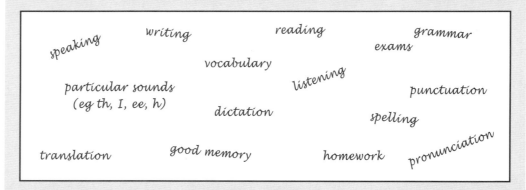

♦ Everyone chooses two or three things they think they're (quite) good at, and they make notes why they are good. What are their strategies? What do they do? How do they think? How do they feel? Do they make pictures in their minds? Do they say things to themselves?

♦ Students find people who are good at the same things as themselves and share strategies. They prepare information sheets about specific skills and give as many suggestions as possible about how to do it well.

♦ Students then work in groups of four – two people who are good at something and two who would like to learn new strategies. The learners try to understand what to do from the information sheet and they ask questions about things they don't understand. They try out the strategies and ask for help when they need more detailed information. All four work on improving the information sheets.

♦ 'Teachers' now become learners of a different strategy, which might mean moving into different groups. They work on a new area in the same way. (It doesn't matter if not everyone teaches and everyone learns, although that is the ideal. The important thing is that everyone works on formulating good learning strategies.)

♦ All the sheets are put up on the walls for everyone to read. Students choose three strategies they will put into practice.

Comment

Even though certain strategies may tend to work better than others for most people, it is wise to remember that we are all individuals and that there is no one definitive right strategy for everybody. A person may have a really bizarre strategy which works for them and for no-one else. Fine. What is important is that it works.

SIMPLE MODELLING

Purpose

For students to discover and try out someone else's strategy for doing something.

Language focus

Describing a procedure/strategy.

PROCEDURE

- Compile with students a shortlist of simple activities to be modelled and write them on the board, eg getting up in the morning, making a decision to do an overdue task, choosing what to order in a restaurant ...

- Students work in pairs. **B** models **A** the first time round. **A** should choose something from the list that they do well and easily – preferably something that **B** is not so good at.

- **B** asks **A** questions to find out exactly how they do that particular thing, eg:

> **B** *I find it really hard to decide what to order in a restaurant. Do you find that easy?*
>
> **A** *Actually I do, yes.*
>
> **B** *So how do you know what to choose?*
>
> **A** *I imagine it in my mind.*
>
> **B** *What do you mean? Do you see a picture?*
>
> **A** *Um... Yes, I suppose it is a picture.*
>
> **B** *What's in the picture?*
>
> **A** *A plate with the food that I'm thinking about.*
>
> **B** *And what happens next?*
>
> **A** *I imagine how I would feel if I ate that.*
>
> **B** *So if it feels good, you go for it. And if it doesn't, you don't. Is that right?*
>
> **A** *Yes, I think that's right. Yes!*
>
> **B** *What sort of feeling? Describe a 'yes' feeling. And a 'no'.*

- **B** feeds back to **A** their complete strategy to check they have it right: *'So what you do first is see a picture of the food and then get a feeling about what it would be like to eat it?'* **B** will need to incorporate any additions or alterations **A** may want to make at this stage.

- As soon as **B** is happy that they understand the strategy, they should imagine themselves in the appropriate situation and run the strategy through in their mind. Does it seem as if it would work? If not, what's missing? What else do they need to know from **A**?

- Get feedback from the whole class as to how the activity went, the difficulties they encountered and the delightful moments they had!

Comment

   An important component of full modelling are the submodalities – the subdivisions of each representational system, such as whether pictures are near or far, in colour or black and white, whether sounds are loud or soft, etc. These can usefully be added to this activity on subsequent occasions

Relating with rapport

Language is more than a collection of words and structures. It is about communication. Learning a new language is learning to relate to people and communicate with them in a new way.

People who communicate well and relate well to other people are said to be *in rapport* with them. All of us relate well to some people, and when we are in rapport with them we do certain things non-consciously. We can help students become aware of what these things are, so that they can do them *consciously* to improve their ability to communicate. This can be useful to all of us if we have to get on with people we don't especially like. It is useful for fostering good relationships within the classroom – which in turn will improve learning. It is particularly useful to language learners who might be feeling nervous or ill-at-ease when using an unfamiliar language in an unfamiliar culture. Once they know what sort of things to look for, they are much better able to integrate into new situations and a new culture.

When people are in good rapport with each other they tend to make a lot of eye contact, have a similar quality of voice, breathe at a similar rate, use the same kind of language, and use the same, or similar body movements. *Matching* and *mirroring* of body movements happens naturally and it is one of the easiest things to do consciously. Strangely, it is usually one of the last things that people notice. Try some activities to raise awareness of rapport:

- Watch videos with students. Choose clips of different people of different ages in different situations (including native speakers) and ask students to identify people who are and who are not in good rapport. (This is often a way of identifying actors who are acting well or not so well, too.)

- Ask students to go 'people watching'. They watch TV. They watch people on public transport, in cafés. They watch friends and family. And they watch themselves and become aware of what they are doing naturally. They report back on their observations.

- Students imagine they are from another planet. Some of their colleagues are going to live on earth. They know nothing about the ways that human beings relate to one another. In groups, students write the 'Top Ten Rules for Getting into Rapport with Earthlings'.

It is important to remember that when we use rapport consciously, the key is making the other person feel good when they are with you – within the bounds of an honest and appropriate relationship. No-one feels good if they think they are being manipulated or being made fun of. Keep classroom practice fun, and gently warn students to treat other people with respect.

Purpose

To practise empathy and rapport building.

Language focus

Mm, Oh, Uh huh.

Oh dear! Really? Poor you! Hard luck! Well done! Congratulations! Wow!

How terrible/awful/dreadful/ghastly/embarrassing/mean/horrible/frightening!

How wonderful/exciting/amazing/thrilling/fascinating/delightful!

What a shame/pity/disappointment/let down/terrible thing to happen!

PROCEDURE

● Elicit the language of empathy.

● Give one of the statement cards to each student. Students mingle and say different sentences (with feeling) to others who respond appropriately.

I've just had six fillings at the dentist!

I came top of the class in maths.

I failed my driving test – again!

Our new English teacher is brilliant.

I came second in the tennis competition.

The cat's just been sick all over the floor!

I've got a new baby sister.

I'm so fed up and depressed.

I've got the most terrible indigestion!

I've passed my driving test.

I had to queue for hours at the post office!

I got a new bike for my birthday.

We're going to Mauritius for our summer holiday.

I've got this terrible pain in my big toe.

I went to a fantastic concert at the weekend.

They were really awful to me at the interview!

BODY MATCH

Purpose

To practise body matching and attentive listening (and questions).

Language focus

Empathetic listening; fluency.

PROCEDURE

- Students prepare to tell their partner an anecdote for about two minutes.
- Students work in pairs. **A** is the speaker, **B** the listener.
- While **A** talks, **B** body matches **A** and shows interest in what **A** is saying with
  - gestures and head nods
  - supportive noises (*Mm, Oh*, etc) – within reason
  - repetition of key words (sparingly and only if appropriate)
  - questions to check information or get more information (if appropriate)

  That is all **B** does. **B** should definitely not give opinions.
- After two minutes, get reactions from the group. How did it feel to listen like that? How did it feel to be listened to in that way?
- Swap roles.

Variation

- Stagger the instructions for showing interest so students concentrate on one strategy at a time, before combining them. This gives additional language practice to the story tellers who can tell the same story to different partners.
- This and the following activity can be done in groups of three, where each pair has an observer whose job it is to watch, listen and report back on the activity. The activity is then three-phase, with everyone taking each role once. Taking the role of observer often gives students valuable reflection time.

VOICE MATCH

Purpose

To practise attentive listening and voice matching.

Language focus

Past simple; fluency and repetition.

PROCEDURE

- Students prepare (mentally or on paper) to tell their partner a short anecdote (maximum of two minutes) – preferably something which happened to them.
- Students work in pairs. **A** tells **B** their short anecdote. **B** concentrates on noticing very precisely what is said, and how it is said.
- **B** sits in **A**'s chair and pretends to be **A**. **B** retells **A**'s story back to **A**, matching **A**'s voice in terms of speed, tone and pitch.
- Feedback on students' reactions – both from the point of view of the talker and the listener, first in pairs, then with the whole class, if appropriate.

MATCH OR MISMATCH

Purpose

Exploring the effects of matching and mismatching body language.

Language focus

Fluency.

PROCEDURE

◆ Divide the class into two groups, **A**s and **B**s.

Give **A**s an instruction which reads:

> Prepare a short anecdote to tell to a partner in the other group. Decide how to use your body and voice to make the story as interesting as possible to your listener.

Give **B**s an instruction which reads:

> Your partner will tell you a story. In the beginning, listen attentively and with full rapport. After about a minute, I will drop a book on the floor as if by accident. At this point, stop listening with rapport and start acting as if you are bored and uninterested.

◆ Go to each group and check that they understand what to do.

◆ When both groups are ready and everyone has found a partner, **A**s start telling their story. After about one minute, drop a book. Stand quietly and notice how listeners show a lack of interest and how speakers react.

◆ **B**s tell **A**s what their task was – and apologise. Students share their reactions, in pairs and as a class.

◆ Give **A**s the chance to finish their stories – and this time **B**s listen with interest!

Comment

We do not usually swap roles for this activity, since much of its effect depends on the element of surprise. However, we try to use the same groups and swap roles when we do PACE AND LEAD BODY POSTURE on the next page.

Purpose

To practice pacing and leading someone's body posture.

Language focus

Language of empathy – see EMPATHETIC RESPONSES (page 121); fluency.

PROCEDURE

- Divide the class into two groups, **A**s and **B**s.
  Give **A**s an instruction which reads:

  > Prepare a short anecdote to tell to a partner in the other group. Decide how to use your body and voice to make the story as interesting as possible to your listener.

  Give **B**s an instruction which reads:

  > Your partner will tell you a story. Listen with full attention and with as much physical rapport as possible. After a few moments, change your body position while continuing to give **A** your full attention. Notice if – after a moment – **A** follows your change.

- Go to each group and check that they understand what to do.
- When both groups are ready, and everyone has found a partner, **A**s start telling their story.
- At the end of the activity, **B**s lead the feedback in their pairs by asking **A**s what they noticed. They then tell **A**s what their task was.
- Whole class discussion.

Comment

Pacing simply means making sure you are in good rapport with someone – before you try to influence (lead) them to do what you want them to do. The trick is to do a lot of pacing before you start leading. And if they don't follow? Then pace some more.

Seek first to understand, then to be understood.

Purpose

To practise verbal pacing and leading.

Language focus

The language of pacing (apologising/acknowledging) and leading (making a tentative or polite request).

PROCEDURE

♦ Students read and/or listen to a dialogue which illustrates verbal pacing and leading, like this:

MOVE THOSE MUDDY BOOTS!

On a train, passenger **B**, sitting facing passenger **A**, is reading the newspaper with their muddy boots up on the seat next to **A**.

A *Excuse me!*

B *Yes?*

A *I'm sorry to interrupt your reading ...*

B *That's OK.*

A *I know you're probably very tired and need to relax, but could I ask if you could possibly put your feet down?*

B *Eh? They're very comfortable up there.*

A *I'm sure they are. The problem is that your boots are muddy, and they're making the seat dirty.*

B *Are they? Oh well, in that case ... (taking them down).*

A *Thank you very much.*

Comment

We know that not all interactions like this have such a happy ending. They do, however, stand a better chance of a positive dénouement, if we pace the other person, rather than accusing them or attacking them.

♦ Discuss with students how **B** managed to be successful. What kind of language did **B** use?

♦ Brainstorm other situations where someone is doing something we would like them to stop doing ... or not doing something we would like them to do, eg:

The neighbours are playing really loud music late at night.

Your friend borrowed your favourite T-shirt ages ago and still hasn't given it back.

The person sitting opposite you is smoking in a non-smoking compartment.

The waitress has forgotten to bring your chips.

♦ Input language if necessary (see next page).

♦ Students work in pairs to script and/or roleplay a situation of their choosing.

Language to input if necessary

◆ Elicit or input useful language for making requests (leading), eg

Tentative polite requests

Can/could you possibly …	*turn the volume down?*
Would you mind (not –ing) …	*letting me have my T-shirt back?*
Do you think you could possibly …	*not smoke, please?*
Would it be (at all) possible for you to …	*bring me my chips?*
I wonder if you could possibly …	*let me have my T-shirt back?*
Would you consider (–ing) …	*smoking in the corridor, do you think?*

The reason for starting with leading is that this language is more likely to be familiar to students.

◆ The language of pacing may be harder to elicit, and could first be done in the students' own language. Ask students if they would go straight into making a request or whether they would say anything else first, eg

Apologising

I'm sorry to interrupt your party/coffee, but …
I'm sorry to be a nuisance/pain/killjoy, but …
I do apologise for interrupting, but …

Acknowledging

I know/realise		*right in the middle of a super party, but …*
I do understand	*that you're*	*really fond of my T-shirt, but …*
I'm very aware		*enjoying your cigarette, but …*
		very busy, but …

BE A MIRROR

Purpose

To help students notice and practise mirroring body movements; to foster a good classroom atmosphere; to get people moving.

PROCEDURE

◆ Students work in pairs. They stand up and face each other. **A** is the 'leader', **B** is the 'follower' or 'mirror'. They put their hands in front of them with the palms close to each other but not touching. **A** moves slowly, **B** mirrors exactly, while maintaining eye contact (and therefore relying solely on peripheral vision).

◆ After a moment, stop and check how they are doing. Remind them how mirrors work if they move towards and away from each other. Keep movements slow.

◆ Swap roles, so **B** is the leader and **A** the follower.

◆ Finally, students do the activity with no designated leader and follower.

◆ Invite feedback from the students on the experience – especially the last phase. (During the final phase there is usually non-explicit turn-taking to be leader.)

Someone else's shoes

First position	Second position	Third position
ME	YOU	NEUTRAL OBSERVER
How I experience something.	How you experience it – or how I imagine you experience it.	How a third person might experience it.

Good communicators seem to have the flexibility to shift easily from one position to another as appropriate. There are times when it's important to know what you want and to go for it (first position); there are times when it's important to be able to imagine what the other person might be experiencing (second position); and there are times when it's important to step out and observe what's happening in a detached way, particularly at moments of conflict (third position).

All three positions are important. A lot of this book is about first position and exploring our own behaviour and thinking processes. We deal with third position whenever we consider situations objectively. The one we explore here in the context of rapport is second position. The ability to second-position another person (or group of people) is a crucial element of rapport.

The activities which follow give students the opportunity to put themselves in someone else's shoes and see things from their point of view. In fact, a good way of broaching the subject is to ask the class to look at the shoes of the person next to them and to imagine what it would be like to have them on their own feet.

Give students the opportunity to put themselves in someone else's footsteps, literally. They work in pairs. The leader goes for a walk (outside the building, if possible), trying to be as natural as possible, walking naturally, noticing what they might normally notice, stopping or moving on as they would usually do. Their partner follows and tries to do exactly what they do. After five minutes, they stop and the follower checks anything they didn't understand and reports on how it felt to 'be' the other person. They then reverse roles. Back in the classroom, everyone discusses what they learnt about themselves and others.

I AM SOMEONE WHO

Purpose

To practise listening skills and to imagine what an experience is like from another person's point of view.

Language focus

The activity is a meaningful, individual drill; *I am someone who -s ...*

PROCEDURE

- Students work in pairs. For one minute **A**s make statements about themselves beginning, *'I am someone who ...'* (eg *I am someone who gets up early, I am someone who hates waiting for a bus.*) **B**s listen carefully using head movements and supportive noises to show interest, imagining what it's like to be **A** saying those things.

- Pairs swap chairs. **B** retells **A** everything they can remember **A** said, putting themselves in **A**'s shoes and using the pronoun 'I': *'I am someone who ...'*

- Whole class feedback. How much did **B** remember? Did it help to 'be' **A**, using the pronoun 'I' and sitting in **A**'s chair?

- **A** and **B** swap roles and do the activity again.

Variation

- **B** can play a more active role by asking each time: *Who are you?* **B** should not make any other comments until the pairs swap chairs.

- The statement can be modified to practise different structures, eg *'I do this'*, *'I like -ing/I don't like -ing'*, *'I can/can't ...'*, *'I have/haven't done ...'* *'I'm/I'm not'* and so on, so it can be used at all levels.

Purpose

To make students aware of how good their second-position skills are already and to give them the confidence to trust their instincts.

Language focus and preparation

Fluency; listening practice; review of past simple and past continuous.

Language of tentative suggestion:

> *As you were speaking, I imagined X happened.*
> *I had a sense of it being very cold/hot/threatening ...*

Language for confirming or (gently) correcting someone's ideas:

> *You were (quite/absolutely) right about X/when you said that ...*
> *You weren't quite right about ... when you said ... but ...*

PROCEDURE

◆ Students work in pairs. **A**s tell **B**s about a wonderful holiday experience they have had. (It needn't be anything exotic, a nice day out somewhere is fine).

◆ **B**s listen using all their matching and listening skills to really sense what **A** experienced and really imagine what it must have been like to be **A**.

Comment

Something that Robert Dilts does to facilitate this kind of second-position listening is to imagine three sets of 'bands' linking you to the other person. One band goes around the back of your head and your partner's head, one band goes around your waists and one joins you at the ankles. You may find it useful to explore this idea yourself, before offering it to your students.

◆ After two minutes, **B**s tentatively fill in gaps in **A**'s description according to how they imagined it as **A** was speaking. **B**s don't just repeat what **A** has said, but add new information that **A** didn't mention. **B** might say: *'I imagined you felt particularly happy that day because of something – maybe some good news'*, or *'I have a sense that you were wearing something green'*, or *'Was there a child who did something?'*

While **B** is speaking, **A** listens without interrupting to correct or contradict **B**.

◆ The story-telling and gap-filling may happen just once, or may be repeated two or three times.

◆ Both **A** and **B** get out of their seats and stand somewhere nearby (in third position). It is at this moment, and this moment only, that **A** can begin to give **B** feedback on their ideas. And when they do this, they should concentrate on what **B** got right rather than what **B** got wrong. **A** might say things like: *'You were absolutely right about the good news ... I'd forgotten'*, or *'I wasn't actually wearing anything green, but everything around was very green because it had been raining a lot.'*

◆ **A**s and **B**s swap roles.

◆ The class share their reactions to the activity.

ROLEPLAY ALL THE PARTS

Purpose

To make students aware of the usefulness of experiencing a situation from a different point of view.

Language focus and preparation

Any, depending on the content of the roleplay, eg language of persuasion, criticism, accusation, etc; chance for repetition in first, second and third person singular; fluency and listening practice.

Some useful language in the roleplay with teenagers might be:

You're grounded for x days.

No allowance/pocket money for x days/weeks.

While you're living in my house you live by my rules.

(This language is probably typical of parents speaking to their children, but is it necessarily the most effective strategy?)

PROCEDURE

♦ Students work in pairs to act out a short roleplay, eg parent complaining to child/teenager about always using the telephone, or about coming home late at night. **A** is the parent, saying the sorts of things a parent would say. **B** sits in the opposite chair and listens as the child, but makes no response.

♦ When **A** can think of nothing more to say, **A** and **B** swap chairs. **A** now speaks in the role of the child responding to the parent, using 'I' as the child and 'you' to the parent. **B** listens as the parent and says nothing.

♦ If **A** wants to add anything to either part, **A** and **B** swap chairs so that **A** only speaks when sitting in the appropriate chair. (**A** swaps chairs and roles as many times as necessary.) **B** listens but doesn't speak.

♦ **A** and **B** stand up and look at the chairs. **A** comments on the interaction. **B** is supportive and helpful, asking questions such as, '*Did the parent and child both say what they wanted to say?*' '*Is there anything they could have said in a better way?*' If asked by **A**, **B** can offer suggestions for how the interaction could have been better handled.

♦ **A** repeats the activity, again taking both roles, aiming for a better outcome.

♦ **A** and **B** discuss the experience together. Main points are shared in a whole-class discussion.

♦ The whole sequence is repeated with **B** taking the active role, with a slightly different situation.

Comment

A better outcome of a conflict is usually achieved if each person expresses clearly what the other person did and how they themselves felt as a result, and states precisely what they would like the other person to do:

When you …, I felt …

I would like you to …

Fostering group rapport

A large part of our role as teachers is to create a supportive environment where learners feel confident and good about themselves and each other, where they feel safe to try things out, take risks, make mistakes – and succeed. These activities are designed to foster such an environment.

CIRCLE OF COMPLIMENTS

Purpose

To encourage students to comment on each other's strengths (rather than their weaknesses); to help students feel good about themselves and each other.

Language focus and preparation

Expressing opinions about other people.

I (really) like/love	the way you smile/laugh/help people/tell jokes …
I (really) like/love	your hair/teeth/hands/sweater/shoes …
You've got a (really) good	sense of humour/accent …
You're (really) good at	spelling/making people laugh/singing …

PROCEDURE

♦ Students sit in a circle with you. A 'special' student is chosen (either by taking names out of a hat, or for a special reason, such as a birthday).

♦ Everyone (including you) takes it in turns to tell the person something they like about them. This does not have to be done in order round the circle. People can speak as and when they are ready to do so.

Comment

This activity can be repeated frequently and might even become part of class routine. Once everyone has been the 'special' person (including the teacher), you can start round again and find new things to say about people.

Variations

♦ Once students have learned how this activity works, on subsequent occasions the class can work in smaller groups.

♦ This can also be done without singling out a particular person, but just leaving it open for anyone to say something nice about anyone in the group. We have found that there seems to be an unspoken group consensus to make sure everyone is covered.

♦ Students might from time to time write their compliments on slips of paper rather than (or as well as) saying them. Alternatively individuals can write their names on a sheet of paper and people go round the room writing compliments to one another – in English.

DISLIKE/LIKE

Purpose

To encourage students to express their feelings and give and receive honest feedback.

Language focus

I (really) dislike/like + present simple ... *or I liked/didn't like ...* + past simple.

PROCEDURE

- Near the end of a lesson, students stand in a circle with you.

- In turn, starting with a volunteer, everyone (including the teacher) makes a statement about the lesson, starting *'I don't/didn't like ...'*, eg *'I didn't like it when people kept talking when other people were speaking.'* Statements can be about anything in the lesson. They are accepted without comment (this may be hard to begin with). Anyone who doesn't want to say something, says *'Pass'.*

- The sequence is repeated with everyone making a statement about the lesson, beginning, *'I (really) appreciated ...'* or *'I (really) like/liked ...'*, eg *'I really liked the way you waited for me to find the words I wanted to say.'* Again statements are accepted without comment and people are allowed to pass.

Comment

Silly or unhelpful comments are relatively few and far between. We have received very helpful feedback on lessons, particularly when students realise that we really do want to know their opinion. We have also received some glowing praise from students which they would not otherwise have had the opportunity to voice. The teacher also has the opportunity to feed back to the class something negative and something positive. Make sure you keep your own comments to one main point – resist the urge to say more, to reply to statements (at the time or later), or to correct the English!

POSITIVE QUESTIONS

Purpose

To encourage students to focus on the positive things in life.

Language focus

Creating questions; past and future.

PROCEDURE

- Students work in groups to generate positive empowering questions, such as, *'What was really special about today?' 'What am I really good at?' 'What am I really looking forward to tomorrow?'*

- Students all look at each group's questions and individually choose and write down the ones that most appeal to them. They check in their groups for correct grammar and spelling.

- Suggest that students put the questions up on their bedroom wall and get into the routine of asking and answering them morning and night.

FAMOUS 'FAILURES'

Purpose
To comfort students by getting them to realise that many successful people didn't come by their success easily, they had a few hiccoughs on the way!

Language focus
Past simple; fluency.

PROCEDURE

♦ Write the names (or display pictures) of these people on the board:

Albert Einstein	Marilyn Monroe	Dustin Hoffman	Walt Disney
Eva Peron	Nelson Mandela	Abraham Lincoln	Thomas Edison
Sylvester Stallone	John Pierpont Morgan		

♦ Students say as much as they can about them and why they are/were famous. Can they guess what they all had in common? (They all started as failures and became successful later.)

♦ In groups, they match each of these statements with one of the people.

    a This person spent 26 years in prison.

    b This person had to work at the age of seven, lost eight elections and all their money.

    c This person came from a very poor family.

    d This person made 17 films before getting a star role.

    e This person was fired by a newspaper for not having any ideas.

    f This person was sacked from his job in a restaurant for eating too much.

    g This person's first job was as a lion-cage cleaner.

    h This person 'failed' to catch the Titanic.

    i This person's maths teacher thought he was useless.

    j This person failed about 1999 times before his invention succeeded.

♦ Can they think of any more successful people who didn't always have it easy?

♦ Can they think of any message that this activity illustrates?

ANSWERS

a = Nelson Mandela b = Abraham Lincoln c = Eva Peron d = Marilyn Monroe e = Walt Disney f = Dustin Hoffman g = Sylvester Stallone h = John Pierpont Morgan (owner of the Titanic) i = Albert Einstein j = Thomas Edison (inventor of the lightbulb)
In addition, Warren Beatty, Jane Fonda and Michael Douglas dropped out of college, Humphrey Bogart and Joan Collins were expelled from school, and Mark Twain went bankrupt.

Purpose

To help learners be aware of the many things they can already do and reinforce their belief in their abilities.

Language focus

Can.

PROCEDURE

- Students make a list of all the things they can do in whatever field, eg *'I can swim.' 'I can make a great paella.' 'I can read a book really fast.'*

- They get together in groups of four or five to find five things in common to all the people in the group. (If they don't reach five things with what they've already written, they go on sharing ideas until they do.) Each time they find a common ability, they stand up and shout, *'Yes, yes, yes!'* and then say what it is they can all do: *'We can all play chess'.*

  This activity either has a time limit, or the activity ends when the first group has found five abilities.

Variation

- Although one doesn't necessarily want to dwell too much on the negative, you could also do this activity with *'can't'.* We sometimes feel that we're the only person in the world who can't do things, so it can be quite comforting and reassuring to discover that other people can't do things either. Have them shout, *'No, no, no!'* (which often makes them laugh about their limitations), and add the word *'yet'* to their negative statement: *'We can't run a marathon – yet!'*

Yes, but ...	*Yes, and ...*
It's all very well saying 'there's no failure, only feedback', but some of my students are going to fail their exams!	• Not necessarily. Our first presupposition is that all our students are going to pass their exams, and we're going to do our best to make that happen. • Every exam has a pass mark. Students are not failures just because they do not achieve that pass mark at the first attempt. • Teaching a language while incorporating NLP does not mean ignoring the realities of life and examinations. One of the goals we set with students is to pass examinations. We prepare students for the exams, make sure that they have sufficient practice of exam conditions in the period leading up to the exam and teach any special techniques which might help them pass exams (including how to relax). However there is a big difference between teaching and testing and most of our time is spent helping students learn English. NLP helps.

Self rapport

If you are not good for yourself, how can you be good for others?

SPANISH PROVERB

Self rapport is sometimes called self esteem. It means taking care of ourselves. It means liking ourselves. It means being as nice to ourselves as we would like other people to be to us. It means talking nicely to ourselves. All too often we talk to ourselves in ways we would never accept from anyone else.

Most importantly, self esteem, or belief in oneself, is probably the most vital element in achieving success at learning – or at anything else in life.

Many of us are very good at remembering and lamenting what we can't do. Oddly enough, it is often easier to praise other people than to praise ourselves. It is important to be acknowledged by others, but it is also important to praise ourselves for the things we do well and which make us feel good. The following activities are designed to do that.

POSITIVE READING BOOK

Purpose
To foster a positive attitude; motivating writing and reading practice.

Language focus
Anything students want to write.

PROCEDURE

- For homework, ask students to notice and write down (in any language) anything good that happens between now and the next lesson and to bring their list to the lesson.

- In the lesson, students work in groups to share the good things that happened to them. They help each other translate their lists into English using dictionaries, or ask you for help. Help them translate what they want to say, even if it is 'beyond' the language level they are at. (With large classes, you might collect in the lists to make sure the English is accurate.)

- Students' accurate work can then be beautifully written, either in individual hardback notebooks, or as a class collection in a book or on the wall.

Comment
Students are much more willing to read things that they have written themselves, and the language will be meaningful because it is what they wanted to say. Do the activity regularly and notice how many more positive things people start noticing when they are looking for them.

Follow up variation

- Students write similar lists where they look for a positive aspect of anything that happens – especially if at first it seems to be something negative.

LIMITING LABELS

Purpose

To help students' challenge the limiting views they hold of themselves.

Language focus

Present simple; past simple.

PROCEDURE

♦ Give each group of four or five students the list of 'labels'. They must make sentences (in the present simple) to say what it is the people actually do. (Some are easier than others).

♦ Share answers (correcting language if necessary).

a singer	*a cook*	*a poet*
a teacher	*a successful person*	*a thief*
an artist	*a good reader*	*a liar*
a failure	*a guitar player*	*a photographer*
a footballer	*a writer*	*a troublemaker*

♦ Groups now try to identify what exactly people did in order to be given the label 'singer' or 'thief'. They write sentences in the present simple or past simple, depending on whether the people did something once or whether they have to do it regularly or professionally in order to acquire the label.

♦ Share answers with the whole group with some language correction where students clearly need help to express what they want to say. Students might also want to use the expression *used to do something* to show that the person still has the label even though they no longer do the activity.

♦ Groups identify what people did or didn't do in order to acquire negative labels, such as *'not a singer'*, *'not a success'*, etc.

♦ Share answers and open up the discussion to cover how and why we label people, how people get stuck with labels, and how people come to believe the labels they are given by themselves and others. What do people need to do in order to change some of the labels they are given?

POSSIBLE ANSWERS

---

a singer sings; a teacher teaches; an artist draws or paints; a failure fails; a footballer plays football; a cook cooks (bakes, fries, prepares food); a successful person succeeds; a good reader reads well; a guitar player plays the guitar; a writer writes; a poet writes poetry (writes poems); a thief steals; a liar lies (tells lies); a photographer takes photographs; a troublemaker makes trouble

Homework

♦ Students make a list of the labels (both positive and negative) they have given themselves or have been given by other people and make notes in response to the following questions:

- *What did you actually do to be given these labels?*
- *Are the labels fair, accurate, helpful to you?*
- *Are there any labels you would like to change?*
- *Start with the unhelpful labels you give yourself. What can you do to change them?*

♦ If you check this homework in class, tell students that they don't have to share any of the precise information about themselves unless they want to, so they should do the activity as honestly as possible. Also ask them to be careful of the feelings of people who do share personal information. Focus principally on the general learning which people took from this activity.

Yes, but ...	Yes, and ...
Why do we have to be positive all the time? Why can't we just be honest and say how things really are? Some things are simply bad. Some people are bad.	• Why is it more honest to say that things are bad? Some things really are good, and some things which seem to be bad, turn out to have a good result in the end. • Some things are bad. You do, though, have a choice about how you react to bad things. NLP gives you some tools to help you change the way you react, if and when you want to. • It may also be that feeling 'bad' about something for a while is a useful and healing emotion, but there comes a time when you want or need to move on. Having strategies to change your state can be very helpful at such times. • As for saying that people are bad, we believe that most people make the best choices they can in the situations in which they find themselves; even if sometimes those choices are not the best for us. Our own behaviour can have a positive influence on the way others behave. However we agree that in the normal course of teaching, there are some people we can help a lot and some on whom we seem to have little effect. As far as we can, we intend to keep acting as if we can make a difference, even if the effects are not immediately visible. • We don't have to be positive all the time. Sometimes we really enjoy being miserable and giving up. And then after a while it's more helpful to look on the bright side and do the best we can in whatever circumstances we find ourselves.

SLOW READER

Purpose

To explore negative labelling.

Language focus

Punctuation; pronunciation.

PROCEDURE

- Give students the poem. Check vocabulary. (A 'server' is a child who gives out things which are needed by the other children in their group.)

- Students work in groups of three and practise reading the poem as they think it is meant to be read. (It should be read slowly and haltingly, one syllable at a time, as if the reader is not very good at reading. If necessary, give a demonstration, and then ask students to practise again.)

- Students rewrite the poem, putting in correct punctuation and capital letters, which will help to check comprehension as well as writing skills. Volunteers write a 'corrected' version on the board for everyone to check their own work.

- Using the rewritten version, students again try to read aloud as slow readers, (which helps them control their pronunciation), and compare that with reading it aloud as fluent readers.

- General class discussion (prepared first in small groups) about the meaning of the poem and their opinion of it.

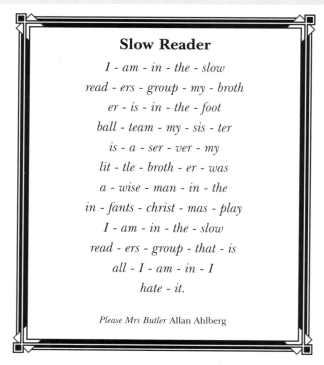

Slow Reader

I - am - in - the - slow
read - ers - group - my - broth
er - is - in - the - foot
ball - team - my - sis - ter
is - a - ser - ver - my
lit - tle - broth - er - was
a - wise - man - in - the
in - fants - christ - mas - play
I - am - in - the - slow
read - ers - group - that - is
all - I - am - in - I
hate - it.

Please Mrs Butler Allan Ahlberg

PUNCTUATED PROSE VERSION   I am in the slow readers' group. My brother is in the football team. My sister is a server. My little brother was a wise man in the infants' Christmas play. I am in the slow readers' group. That is all I am in. I hate it.

LOOSENING LABELS

Purpose

To help students explore more liberating alternatives to unhelpful labels.

Language focus

Substituting verbs for adjectives and nouns; using emphasis and stress to qualify what someone has said.

PROCEDURE

- Remind students what Henry Ford said, '*Whether you think you can or you think you can't, you're right*'. Stress how important it is to shake off limiting labels and to open doors for ourselves by describing ourselves more positively.

- Students match the 'limiting labels' with the 'liberating alternatives'. Ask higher level students to invent alternatives before they see the suggestions. Or students do the task as a communication gap exercise, where one student has the labels and the other has the alternatives.

- Pairs volunteer to check answers aloud for the whole class, emphasising the stress on the words in bold in the liberating alternatives.

Optional follow up

- Ask students to notice every time they label themselves in this way and to explore ways of loosening these labels.

- They work individually or in small groups to write some of their own limiting statements and also think of helpful alternatives, deciding which word(s) to stress in the challenge. Students take it in turns to read out a statement. They invite other group members to suggest more liberating alternatives and then compare these with their own ideas. Remind them that the aim is to be helpful to the person making the limiting statement, not simply to challenge them.

LIMITING LABELS	LIBERATING ALTERNATIVES
1 I'm a failure.	a I haven't produced a masterpiece yet, but **some** of my pictures are quite good.
2 I'm no good at maths.	b I didn't enjoy **that** poem. I wonder if there are other poems I might enjoy more?
3 I'm terribly slow.	c I don't have to be a **professional** singer in order to enjoy singing.
4 My pronunciation is terrible.	d I didn't do **that** very well, but I'm good at lots of other things.
5 I can't draw.	e I've made **one or two** mistakes. That's all part of the learning process.
6 I'm so stupid.	f I'm doing **this** slowly and carefully. I'll get quicker with practice.
7 I hate poetry.	g I didn't understand **that** concept, so I didn't do the exercise very well. I can get help and work on it.
8 I'm not a singer.	h I need to work on it, but I do pronounce **some** things well.

A<small>NSWERS</small>   1-d 2-g 3-f 4-h 5-a 6-e (or g) 7-b 8-c

Purpose

To heighten students' awareness of the negative power of modal verbs and to explore ways of challenging them.

Language focus

Modals.

PROCEDURE

♦ Students work in groups of four or five to complete the following limiting statements with different modals.

should - shouldn't - 've got to - can't - need to - ought to - ought not to - must - mustn't
I .... *wear yellow.*
I .... *eat chocolates.*
I .... *lose weight.*
I .... *get some new trainers.*
I .... *pass this exam.*
I .... *go.*
I .... *study.*
I .... *laugh so loudly.*
I .... *be late.*
I .... *be more mature.*

Suggested challenges

What would happen if you did?

Who says?

What's the worst that would happen if you didn't?

Be more precise.

How much?

How important is this really?

The question not to ask is *'Why?'* This tends to lead to justification of the statement and therefore increases its strength.

♦ In groups of four or five, students think of things they could say to challenge the statements. The aim of the activity is to get the ideas into proportion and be realistic about what really matters and to recognise which things are self-imposed and create unnecessary stress.

Follow up

♦ Ask students to think of their own self-imposed pressures – and to challenge them. This can be done in groups, or set as thought-provoking homework.

Comment

Remind students that they always have a choice. Even if they choose to do something unpleasant in order to have other benefits or to avoid even greater unpleasantness, it is still a choice not to accept the alternatives.

--- SUGGESTED ANSWERS ---

I can't wear yellow. I shouldn't eat chocolates. I need to lose weight. I need to get some new trainers. I must pass this exam. I've got to/I should go. I must/should study. I shouldn't laugh so loudly. I mustn't be late. I ought to be more mature. (Other answers may be possible.)

NEGATIVE WEEK/POSITIVE WEEK

Purpose

An experiment to investigate the power of the media.

Language focus

Anything students want to write.

PROCEDURE

- Ask students for their commitment to undertake an experiment in their free time. For one week, they should try to watch and read (in films, videos, TV programmes, newspaper and magazine articles, etc) about only negative, unpleasant and violent things – in English, if possible. If there is something nice they would like to watch, they record it and wait until the following week. At the end of the week everyone reports back in class, describes the sorts of things they watched and read and anything they noticed about how they felt.

- For the second week they should watch and read only pleasant and positive things. Again, at the end of the week, they share feedback.

- After the experiment and their own feedback, they might be interested to know that previous guineapigs reported that in the 'negative' week, they felt fairly miserable and almost everyone they met was unpleasant and bad tempered, while in their positive week they felt much happier and everyone around them seemed pleasant and good natured. A case of seeing what you're looking for?

Yes, but …	*Yes, and …*
Whatever you still want to write in this space!	• If you've read the whole book and tried everything and you've still got some 'yes buts', then you're probably right. This is reality, and although ultimately we believe that everything is possible if you want it enough, some goals are just not feasible for everyday life. We haven't got all the answers – yet! • If you seriously have another 'Yes, but …' or anything else you'd like to share with us, we'd seriously like to hear about it. Please write to us at Saffire Press.

And I just want you to
remember one more thing:
that everything great that has ever
happened to humanity
since the beginning
has begun as a single thought
in someone's mind.

And if any one of us
is capable of
such a great thought,
then all of us
have the same capacity.

Yanni *Live at the Acropolis*

Index/Contents

─────── KEY ───────

SETTING GOALS	Main section
*Personal profile	Activity
VISUAL DISCRIMINATION	Sub-heading
Climbing a mountain	Story or Guided fantasy
Visual input	Other

Acknowledgements

We would like to thank all those who have contributed to this book in some way. Although all the activities are ones we have 'invented' for use with students at various times, we acknowledge that there is nothing new under the sun, and certainly the following people might recognise variations on some of the exercises: Claudio Borges da Silva, Philip Dale, Chris De Loose, Tim Murphey, John Norman, Hugh Pike, Mario Rinvolucri, Paul Smith, Murray White and Jim Wingate.

Our thanks (again) to Mal Peet for the cartoons on pages 20, 92, 101 and 127, to John Plumb for the 'Spot the Difference' pictures on page 29, and to Tamsin L'Estrange for the Christmas Mind Map on page 34. Mind Maps® are the Registered Trade Mark of the Buzan Organisation, used here with enthusiastic permisssion. (Buzan Centres Ltd, 54 Parkstone Road, Poole, Dorset BH15 2PG, UK. T +44 (0)1202 674676, F +44 (0)1202 674776, buzan@mind-map.com). Brain Gym® (p 46) is the Registered Trade Mark of the Educational Kinesiology Foundation (UK contact: 12 Golders Rise, Hendon, London NW4 2HR. T +44 (0)208 202 3141, F +44 (0)208 202 3890). Thanks also to Zedcor Inc., Tucson, Arizona for the Desk Gallery and ArtToday images on pages 5, 43, 76, 77 and 142. Other artwork and the photos we provided ourselves.

Thanks to Allan Ahlberg for allowing us to use his moving poem on page 138. We thoroughly recommend the other poems in his book 'Please, Mrs Butler', Kestrel, 1983, ©Allan Ahlberg; reproduced by permission of Penguin Books Ltd.

A very big THANK YOU to Hugh L'Estrange for his wonderful job on the design and layout, to Julia Vinton for the beautiful cover and to Rosine Faucompré for her patience and her skill in managing the printing.

And, of course, our thanks to Richard Bandler, John Grinder, Judith de Lozier and all the other NLP pioneers, who continue to expand our understanding.